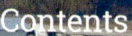

Contents

Contents
4	The Early Years
26	Depot Heydays 1968-1983
56	What Depots do
60	Sectorisation
78	Privatisation
88	Stratford Open Day 1983
96	Depots Today

Depot Features
14	Finsbury Park
18	Tinsley
34	Old Oak Common
40	Eastfield
46	Toton
66	Inverness
72	Penzance
82	Carlisle Kingmoor
90	Cardiff Canton

Welcome

The diesel depot seems to have been around for ever, but in fact the concept is a relatively young one, with dedicated facilities appearing from the late 1950s onwards. This special *Railway Illustrated* publication takes an in-depth look at the development and life of the diesel depot, from the sharing of steam sheds through to the generic types that sprung up across the British Railways network in the 1960s. The story continues through sectorisation in the 1980s and into the privatised era. Specific depots are covered in detail, include three of the largest, Toton, Tinsley and Eastfield. Without doubt the unsung heros of the corporate BR years, they maintained a wonderful mix of loco types; we hope you enjoy this celebration of the diesel depot.

ABOVE: An aerial view of the UK's largest diesel depot at Toton in April 2009; note the large numbers of stored DB Schenker (now DB Cargo) Class 60s. (Andy Martin)

COVER IMAGE: Class 40 40173 awaits its next duty outside Eastfield Depot, the largest facility in Scotland, during the 1970s. (Gavin Morrison)

Editor: Mark Nicholls
Written by: Alex Fisher
Design: Froggatt Designs

Editorial Address
Railways Illustrated,
Key Publishing, PO Box 100,
Stamford, Lincolnshire, PE9 1XQ
Tel: 01780 755131
Web: www.railwaysillustrated.com

Advertising Sales Manager:
Sam Clark
Email: sam.clark@keypublishing.com
Tel: 01780 755131

Advertising Production:
Cheryl Thornburn
cheryl.thornburn@keypublishing.com
Tel: 01780 755131 Fax: 01780 757261

Subscription/Mail Order
Key Publishing Ltd, PO Box 300,
Stamford, Lincs, PE9 1NA
Tel: 01780 480404 Fax: 01780 757812
Subscriptions email: subs@keypublishing.com
Mail Order email: orders@keypublishing.com
Website: www.keypublishing.com/shop

Publishing
Managing Director and Publisher: Adrian Cox
Commercial Director: Ann Saundry
Group Marketing Manager: Martin Steele
Webmaster: Simon Russell
Executive Chairman: Richard Cox

Key Publishing Ltd
PO Box 100,
Stamford,
Lincolnshire, PE9 1XP
Website: www.keypublishing.com

Colour Origination: Froggatt Designs
Printing by: Warner's (Midland) plc, The Maltings, Bourne, Lincs, PE10 9PH
Distribution: Seymour Distribution Ltd, 2 Poultry Avenue, London, EC1A 9PU
Enquiries Line: +44 (0)207 429 4000

We are unable to guarantee the bonafides of any of our advertisers. Readers are strongly recommended to take their own precautions before parting with any information or item of value, including, but not limited to, money, manuscripts, photographs or personal information in response to any advertisements within this publication.

© Key Publishing Ltd 2017
All rights reserved. No part of this magazine may be reproduced or transmitted in any form by any means, electronic or mechanical, including photocopying, recording or by any information storage and retrieval system, without prior permission in writing from the copyright owner. Multiple copying of the contents of the magazine without prior written approval is not permitted.

THE DIESEL DEPOT | 03

The Early Years

The Early

Humble beginnings

After the 1888 use of an internal combustion engine mounted on a truck to demonstrate its practical use, the development of the diesel locomotive was painfully slow. The North Eastern Railway used a two-axle shunting loco at Hull docks in 1894 and with that and other examples that followed came the requirement for their servicing and maintenance. Naturally the first shunters were serviced with only the most rudimentary of facilities. Elevated barrels of fuel dispensing via hoses directly into a tank usually sufficed and, if the loco was fortunate, some kind of covered accommodation or segregated area of a steam shed may have been found.

In 1939 Carlisle Kingmoor had ten diesel shunters and Crewe South, Willesden and Toton had similar numbers. At the time a plan existed for a purpose-built diesel repair shop at Toton. It was to have two roads and be of a near-square shape, 48ft wide by 50ft long, but it was never built. However, the London Midland and Scottish had set up a diesel locomotive maintenance shop prior to September 12, 1947 at Derby Works. Even in those formative years of the diesel depot, it was noted by the authorities that 'conditions in a steam locomotive shop or shed are not favourable to efficient repair or maintenance work on diesel locos' – prophetic words that were still being learned the hard way 20 years later.

The maintenance shop was a 450ft long partitioned off bay section of the paint shop and had two 50 ton travelling cranes with auxiliary hoists of ten ton capacity. Most noticeable was the attention paid to the working environment, with a wooden floor, white lines to denote the gangways and new florescent lighting installed on the walls, along with illuminated pits and the addition of single- and three-phase power supply points for hand-held lamps and equipment. It undertook repairs classified as 'General' every 60,000 miles or seven to eight years that saw a complete rebuild of the loco, a 'Service' at 25,000 to 30,000 miles that was essentially an overhaul of the engine, and finally a 'Casual Repair' that was undertaken as

The Early Years

ABOVE: This image of Aberdeen Ferryhill (61B), taken on July 17, 1965, shows the difficulty BR had in keeping steam and diesels apart. From left to right are LMS Class 5 44797, WD Class 8F 90640, LNER Class A4 60006, LNER Class V2 60836, EE Type 4 D358, BRCW Type 2 D5329, EE Type 4 D265 and BRCW Type 2 D5319. (Bill Wright)

Years

required and encompassed anything deemed out of the scope of the home shed. To accommodate the growing number of shunters in service, some places, such as Parkeston, eventually received purpose-built diesel sheds to house the half a dozen Class 04s that had arrived by 1954.

On December 31, 1947 the LMS had 47 diesel shunters at work in Brent, Crewe, Beeston, Toton and Bescot yards. With the allocation of 10000 and 10001 in December 1947 and July 1948 respectively, followed by a brief allocation of the Southern Region's 1Co-Co1 locomotives 10201 and 10202 in 1951, and finally Fell loco 10100 in January 1952 to November 1958, Derby's diesel locomotive maintenance shop ought to be considered as one of the pioneers of the diesel depot concept; it could also turn out new-build diesels.

The early main line diesels

The allocation of 10000/1 and 10800 to Willesden in January 1948, November 1948 and November 1950 saw the North London facility clean out its best roads around the turntable and paint 'diesels only' clearly on the wall of the turntable pit. This marked Willesden out as another early pioneer in the development of the diesel depot. However, painting 'diesels only' certainly didn't stop steam engines being stabled on the specified roads, and in an effort to obtain more consistent servicing facilities for the diesel fleet, the authorities decided in early 1953 to concentrate 10000/1 and 10201/2 at Nine Elms. They were all there from March and April 1953 and were joined in April 1954 by 10203. Given that Nine Elms had roughly 90 steam engines, the diesels' availably was worse than before, unsurprisingly.

In the spring of 1955, instructions were issued that the diesels were to return to the London Midland Region, and by July 1955 their brief spell at Nine Elms was over. They were concentrated back at Camden shed where they resided amongst its 50 or so steam engines. Their residence coincided with the introduction of some of the first modernisation scheme diesels in the form of BR/Sulzer Type 2s and English Electric Type 4s. When EE Type 1s and BR/Sulzer Type 4s arrived shortly afterwards, the LMS and SR diesels were re-allocated to Willesden.

THE DIESEL DEPOT | 05

The Early Years

| LMR Diesel and Steam Availability, January 1 – September 30, 1957 |||||
Diesel Loco	Days in works	Days on shed	Days worked	Mileage
10000	70	43	148	80,636
10001	76	48	155	83,861
10201	62	30	181	104,532
10202	44	39	190	111,513
10203	84	35	153	74,865
Steam Loco	Days in works	Days on shed	Days worked	Mileage
BR Class 8P	24	58	148	39,709
Coronation 4-6-2	30	41	159	56,800
7 MT 4-6-2	30	42	160	43,158
7P 4-6-0	35	45	150	41,314
Jubilee 4-6-0	22	41	167	45,503

The accompanying table shows how the first mainline diesels were faring. It should be noted that this was before properly equipped diesel sheds were in use and that the diesels listed were not standard types, unlike the steam engines listed. It may be seen that while the number of days in works was disappointing, and the number of days on shed was similar to the steam counterparts, the diesels did twice as many miles. On March 23, 1958 11.1% of BR's 707 diesel-electric locos were out of use, compared with 9.8% for the same time the previous year. The situation was worse for diesel-hydraulic and diesel-mechanical examples, which had 13.3% of their number out of use, although that was a slight improvement upon the 14.7% of the previous year.

Steam depots conversion

Post World War Two and nationalisation, British Railway's decrepit network was concentrated on catching up with the backlog of maintenance and coping with the day-to-day toil of running trains. Steam loco building was pursued with zeal, and while some thought was given to the advances of diesel traction, actually planning for its introduction and making practical progress were slow. In 1953 the Eastern Region sought to have Ipswich steam shed demolished and rebuilt. With commendable forethought, the inclusion of a concrete floor and three levels in the new depot made it one of the first to be built with diesels in mind. Also built very much with a future diesel conversion in mind was Thornaby, which ironically was the last BR depot built for steam.

The £1,250,000 shed opened on June 5, 1958. It was designed to handle 220 locos, with accommodation under cover for 80, and it had an allocation of 148 steam engines. The depot was laid out exceptionally well – for steam, that is – and included such anachronistic features as an octagonal roundhouse, two 70ft turntables, a 350-ton mechanical coaling plant and a high-pressure hot water system for washing out boilers. The only real concession to diesels was the inclusion of a partition wall separating the five-road 'repair shop' and two short roads for the maintenance of 350hp diesel shunters. Somewhat inconveniently, the three diesel fuelling points were sited on the dead-end roads, which wasn't a problem for infrequent use by shunting engines, but wasn't the best design for rapid fuelling of dozens of engines.

In the early 1950s BR decided that it would be wise to separate the day-to-day running of steam locos from the main works and heavier repair facilities. Thus, in an act of folly, in 1954 it decided to construct a new building at Crewe specifically for steam loco mileage examinations and heavy repairs, to be known as the Examination and Repair Depot. The 280ft by 141ft double-ended depot was capable of maintaining the entire LMR allocation to the western line sheds. It consisted of five through roads and five 80ft bays, three at one end and two at the other. The two bays at the north end had a two and a half ton overhead travelling crane and sole bar height platforms for the maintenance of diesel shunting locos, which at the time were being maintained in Crewe South steam shed. Reflecting the depot's primary role for steam maintenance, there was the inclusion of space for a blacksmith, coppersmith and white metal worker. The building was also to have the very best in modern facilities for its workers, including showers, wash rooms and mess facilities for up to 100 men. By 1958 the depot's drawings were entitled 'Alterations for Diesels', the axle journal lathe had been cancelled, an Atlas under-floor machine for re-profiling wheel sets had replaced the wheel drop, diesel tanks capable of holding 14,000 gallons had been added, along with a powered 2½ ton electric travelling crane to the south end of the shed.

Stoke to Derby services commenced DMU operation on September 16, 1957, and from at least November that year they were receiving scheduled maintenance in 'Crewe Diesel Depot'. In early 1958, English Electric Type 4s were visiting the depot for larger examinations, covering 125-150 engine hours and upwards. The former steam depots, North and South, still carried out minor servicing, fuelling and running repairs of diesels.

The Pilot scheme diesels

Contracts for mainline diesels announced in 1955 totalled 174 locomotives, ranged from 800hp to 2,300hp,

BELOW: The first BR depot to have an all-diesel allocation was Devons Road in East London, although initially it was still home to several steam locos, as depicted in this image taken on August 31, 1957. (Brian Morrison)

RIGHT: Norwich Thorpe was one of the earliest depots built purely with diesels in mind, albeit some of the first DMUs. Several early Metropolitan Cammell DMUs (led by E79266) share the new building in 1955. (Chris Booth Collection)

BELOW RIGHT: Glorious image of Camden shed on August 10, 1962 with three EE Type 4s (including D214 nearest the camera). The problem of providing clean facilities for diesels is obvious. (Rail Photoprints/Dave Cobbe)

The Early Years

to be used on the London Midland, Eastern and Western Regions of BR. Increased orders meant that 50 of the 230 main line locos were expected to be delivered during 1957, and more than 100 in 1958, in addition to 500 new diesel shunters.

Sir Brian Robertson, Chairman of the British Transport Commission, claimed in March 1957 that the pace of BR modernisation would increase rapidly from 1958, and more than one-third of the £1.2bn to be spent under the scheme was committed to various projects. The spending included £92m for electrification, £33.5m for main line diesels and shunting locos, £32m for DMUs and £46m for major works, such as track widening, new junctions and stations, and depot re-construction schemes – note the use of the term depot re-construction and not new facilities. Despite the large orders in place and the impending diesel deliveries, plans for depots seemed scant, especially in comparison to the new purpose-built EMU and DMU depots that were rapidly appearing, such as those at St Leonards, Buxton and Darlington.

The first all-diesel depots

Perhaps the first depot created exclusively for shunters, diesel railcars and later main line diesels, was the

The Early Years

conversion of Leith passenger station in 1955. The station closed on April 7, 1952 and its large overall 206ft long roof made it a useful space for the accommodation of DMUs and locos. The depot went on to have allocations of NBL Shunters and Class: 05, 06, 08, 20, 24, 26 and 40, along with visits from Deltics.

When the first of the Pilot Scheme locomotives, English Electric Type 1 D8000, was handed over to the BTC on June 2, 1957 it underwent trials at Derby before being allocated to Devons Road, Bow, which was being transformed into the first all-diesel depot in Britain. BR hoped the three-road dead-end facility would provide valuable experience that would assist in planning the future conversion to full diesel servicing of other depots due for alteration. By November 1957, fuel oil storage tanks, fuelling equipment and subsidiary alterations to the permanent way, drainage and paving had been undertaken. Inspection pits were deepened and fitted with lights; a workshop and store were also provided, along with modern heating and lighting throughout the building. The depot was designed to cater for 15 mixed traffic locos of 1,000hp, ten mixed traffic engines of 800hp, six 300hp and two 350hp shunters. As a hang over from steam, the depot had four roads known as the 'stabling shed', which were for little more than parking engines under cover – something of a luxury for diesels that was later deemed superfluous. At this time other depots were also having alterations to accommodate diesels, such as Manchester Longsight's south shed where pits were widened and equipped with fluorescent lighting.

The first of an initial order of 1,250hp A1A-A1A Brush Type 2s was ceremoniously handed over to the ER at the maker's Loughborough Works on October 31, 1957. The 20 locos on were all based at Stratford in East London,

ABOVE LEFT: Originally numbered 7087, former LMS 350hp 0-6-0 shunter 12010 stands inside the roundhouse at Toton on May 17, 1953. The small class was built between 1939 and 1942 and some served abroad during World War Two with the War Department. (Darren Fearson Collection)

RIGHT: Instructions to keep diesel and steam locos separate at Willesden Depot were not always adhered to, as in this image of BR/Sulzer Type 2s D5026, D5077 and Black Five 45280 in the roundhouse in 1964. (Rail Photoprints/Gordon Edgar Collection, A E Durrant)

BELOW: Steam locos share the shed at Grangemouth with several BR 0-6-0 shunters on July 18, 1965. (Bill Wright)

The Early Years

The Early Years

for which the ER made the contentious claim of being "the first purpose-built Diesel Maintenance Depot". Although it opened in 1958 as a diesel depot, it was built with the intention of being turned over to DMU and shunting locos once a planned four-road double dead end, 300ft maintenance shed was completed. By January 1959 there were 30 diesels in the railcar shed, and as Dick Hardy, head of the Stratford District at the time, stated: "We were failing to maintain or clean them properly, the railcar shed was overcrowded and unsuitable." He added: "There was a critical shortage of fitters and, above all, electricians."

Through a self-taught boilermaker's suggestion, an unofficial training school was set up at Stratford to convert boilermakers and fitters to electricians. In July 1958, an official school was set up by the CM&EE in Stratford Works. BR belatedly concluded that proper schools for the tutoring and education of trained staff to maintain the new diesels were required and these duly spread throughout Britain, in many cases after the diesels had started to arrive.

Regional variations

In 1957, the Chief Operating Superintendent of the Western Region stated in a paper entitled *The Outlook on the Modern Railway Operation*, that the extensive dieselisation of the WR would take place by geographical area, with steam power replaced by diesels in the shortest possible time before the next was tackled, to avoid working steam and diesel power side by side. The first stage of the scheme was to see services west of Exeter (except the former Southern lines) dieselised by the end of 1959. The centre of the project was to be Laira Depot at Plymouth.

On the ER the new Ipswich depot building opened on November 2, 1959, with the authorities claiming it to be the first on British Railways to become all diesel. Technically, four days later BR Class J19 0-6-0 no 64641 became the last steam loco to be repaired at Ipswich, and from then on only diesels were dealt with. The six-road building had four roads for servicing and two for maintenance. It should be noted that as the two roads in the maintenance shed had a central platform to create four separate berths, Ipswich ought to be considered as the ER's first double ended, dead end shed, albeit in a small way. Ipswich's allocation quickly grew to 62 Type 2s, along with maintenance responsibility for Parkeston Quay's shunters. The depot had 200 drivers and 80 maintenance staff, with those in the servicing shed undertaking fuelling and inspections, while maintenance shed staff undertook weekly, monthly and three-monthly inspections/exams. Cyclical working of its Type 2s over six-day rosters ensured the machines returned to Ipswich for scheduled maintenance.

There was even a proposal to build a 210ft three-road diesel maintenance shed nearby, with a possible 240ft extension, presumably in the ER style similar to Frodingham Depot. However, such forward thinking was undermined when, fewer than ten years after becoming diesel only, Ipswich undertook its final loco repair on May 5, 1968, on a Class 15. The building continued to be used, although fuelling was transferred to a point adjacent to the station.

Purpose-built diesel depots

The ER's drive to dieselisation meant it was the greatest exponent of the standard diesel facility, and steel-framed Finsbury Park is considered to be BR's first purpose-built diesel depot. It was designed and built under the general direction of A K Terris, the Chief Civil Engineer, and opened in April 1960. Its six roads could each hold three locos – an Achilles heel that made the planning of exams all the more important if locos were not to be trapped inside. Subsequent ER sheds reduced berths to two per road.

Despite being the most progressive in their eradiation of steam, some ER depots were still dual worked for a

Depots loco allocation, October 7, 1961

Eastern (400)	London Midland (251)	Southern (87)	Western (118)				
122	Stratford	49	Derby	87	Hither Green	79	Laira
99	Finsbury Park	40	Willesden			22	Newton Abbot
52	Darnall	38	Camden			17	Bristol Bath Road
52	Ipswich	28	Crewe				
52	March	24	Longsight	North Eastern (114)	Scottish (178)		
23	Norwich	22	Cricklewood	58	Gateshead	61	Eastfield
		19	Devons Road	22	Neville Hill	48	Inverness
		17	Edge Hill	20	York	37	Haymarket
		10	Carlisle Upperby	14	Thornaby	25	Kittybrewster
		3	Watford			7	Polmadie
		1	Newton Heath				

ABOVE RIGHT: A Brush Type 2 receives attention at Ipswich Depot on November 6, 1959. The depot was purpose-built for diesels, as is evident from the inspection pit, raised track and overhead platform. (NRM)

BELOW RIGHT: In later life, some purpose-built diesel depots found new leases of life, such as the former shed at Lincoln that was used by the local bus company on May 13, 1996. (Chris Booth)

BELOW: BRCW Type 3s D6573 and D6579 share the roads outside Hither Green Depot with shunter Ds1173 on March 7, 1965. (Rail Photoprints/John Chalcraft)

The Early Years

number of years. At March steam shed, roads 1 and 2 were dedicated to diesel shunters, and as main line diesels arrived, maintenance and repairs took place on the first four roads, which were partitioned off. Inspection and fuelling of 40 Brush Type 2s was taking place without spillage trays in the timber-beamed steam shed until the ER built a standard depot, which entered service in November 1963.

Finsbury Park had set a design standard that was perpetuated throughout the ER at Colchester, Frodingham, Hitchin, Immingham, Lincoln, March, Shirebrook, Stratford, Tinsley and Wath. Terris insisted on traditional pitched roofs up to a gable, as he maintained this would help to disperse diesel exhaust fumes.

Devons Road, BR's first all-diesel depot, closed on February 10, 1964 and its allocation of D2900-D2906 and D8013-19 was transferred to Willesden and Stratford. It had outlived its usefulness and replacing it were new depots that were bright, airy and better equipped. Washing plants were deemed a necessity rather than a useful extra, and the depots' dead end roads were restricted to a maximum of two loco lengths. Tinsley perhaps represented the zenith of this 1960s design when it fully opened in April 1964. By 1965 its allocation had grown to 159, with an admirable 85% availability rate. With the ER concentrating its locos at eight main maintenance depots, its fleet of 1,200 was spread at an average of 150 per depot. While contemporary reports suggested this was too high, with 90-100 being suggested as a more manageable number, several other depots, such as the LMR's Toton and Scotland's Eastfield, also had huge fleets. Such was the difference in maintenance requirements of diesels, in August 1962 the unions were informed that the swift elimination of steam meant 19,000 workshop staff would be redundant over a five-year period.

The issue of provisions for servicing and maintenance is one on which the BR regions had stark differences of opinion. On the WR, and even more so on the ER, the two were seen as firmly divided functions. At Tinsley the two buildings were completely separate, with the servicing shed being down in the yard complex far away from the main depot, and it was the same at Old Oak Common, although they were closer together. On the LMR, its major depot at Toton sited the fuelling and servicing shed alongside the maintenance building. However, elsewhere on the LMR there were some larger depots built to a generic style, such as Wigan and Carlisle Kingmoor.

Conclusion

By the late 1960s a consensus of opinion labelled BR's rapid eradication of steam as imprudent. Views expressed at the time were that BR had been "dazzled by visions of the high potential economies of diesel traction and the glitter of money after so many lean years". BR was so fixated upon the rapid expulsion of steam that the pace of introduction of replacement diesels was heavily weighted towards numbers, but decidedly underweighted towards service proving, operating and maintenance staff training. Perhaps most significant was the under-provision of a specialised maintenance and repair organisation. Such an approach is hard to fathom when the relative costs of new diesels and their steam counterparts in the late 1950s was so startling. Steam ranged in price from as low as £14,627 for a 2-6-2T, through to £20,000-plus for a 4-6-2, and up to £33,497 for a 2-10-0 9F. Diesels ranged in price quite considerably with an EE Type 1 costing £58,955, through to a BR/Sulzer Type 4 costing £144,422, although the more numerous EE Type 4 cost 'only' £106,807. Reports from the early 1960s lay clear the deficiencies of some of the early main line types, especially the in-service failures and high rates of unreliability. In the early diesel years, BR garnered only negligible advantages and economies, but in 1963, nearly a decade after diesels' introduction, BR produced a report which showed that the economies inherent in them were not just a chimera.

Diesels reduced the number of men required at a depot for cleaning and coaling engines and there was also a reduction in train crew required for re-manning trains. It was possible on the GE section of the Eastern to achieve a ratio of 3.1 crew members to one loco. Steam crews averaged a mere 76 miles per turn of duty, but with diesels the mileage rose to 124, with an average rostered time in movement of four hours 40 minutes per turn. Economic gains expanded almost in proportion to the growth of staff familiarisation with the new fleet. New techniques and tools were developed as well, but, perhaps most importantly, in 1966, Mr G T Smithyman, BR's first Chief Mechanical Engineer, developed standardised maintenance schedules. In collaboration with the regional CMEs, he collated and pooled the knowledge and experience that existed around the regions to the great benefit of BR's diesel fleet. Finally, while traffic losses and line closures accounted for some of the reductions, the changeover from steam to diesel lowered loco numbers by 75% and a large number of motive power depots were closed. By the end of 1966 all of the major depots were built and if not already open soon would be, even if, in most cases, it was several years after diesels had come to their areas. Vividly apparent, however, was that the lack of clear and rigid guidance from the BR board that had meant the regions had been free to pursue different approaches to the styling and composition of maintenance and servicing depots.

Finsbury Park
Britain's first all-new diesel depot

As iconic depots go, Finsbury Park is right up there. It holds the accolade for being the first purpose-built diesel depot on BR, and with its Deltics famously receiving white cab embellishments, it was certainly one of the best-known. It was situated on the site of the old Clarence Yard goods sidings and built to the then-standard Eastern Region (ER) design of a steel frame and an expanse of glass, as directed by the Chief Civil Engineer and Architect for the ER. Its steelwork was by Wright Anderson & Co of Gateshead, and general construction by Wimpey & Co. Built in 1959, it opened on April 24, 1960 with Tom Greaves as the manager. It had a single span roof of 111½ft over six roads, each holding three locos. It was designed to maintain up to 180 locos, including 31 diesel shunters.

The adjoining two-storey workshop contained offices, stores, small electric tools, air filter cleaning, battery charging and injector testing facilities. The rails in the servicing shed were raised 2ft 6in and were supported by pillars 5ft apart. A lower pit between the rails allowed staff to work on bogies and traction motors. Concrete platforms 7ft above the main floor level ran the length of the shed between adjacent tracks and obviated the need for portable platforms to reach a loco's footplate. Supplies of water, oil and compressed air were also piped to several dispensing points between each track.

Notably, the depot was designed to permit extensions for electric locos and, importantly, while it had servicing facilities these were ostensibly for periodic maintenance, with servicing and running repairs to be done at King's Cross, Hornsey, Hatfield and Hitchin. The three locos per road had to be positioned so that the first in was the one requiring the greatest amount of work and so was the last out to avoid troublesome shunting of engines still under examination.

The first locos

Finsbury Park's initial allocation came mainly from nearby Hornsey Depot, which then reverted to all-steam and became a sub shed of Finsbury Park from 1961 until its closure in May 1971. Upon opening, Finsbury Park had 12 BR 0-6-0 350hp shunters (later Class 08), five LMS/BR 0-6-0 350hp shunters (Class 11), 13 English Electric Type 1s (Class 20), 10 EE Type 2s (Class 23 'Baby Deltics'), 12 BRCW Type 2s (Class 26), 24 Brush Type 2s (Class 31) and six EE Type 4s (Class 40). The BRCW Type 2s had moved on by October 1960 and two BTH Type 1s (Class 15), D8237 and D8238, arrived in November and December 1960 respectively.

Two BRCW Type 3s (Class 33), D6504 and D6559, spent a month each, February and December 1961 respectively, at Finsbury Park. The former came for tests to its ETH equipment and the latter for crew training so that the type could be used on the Cliffe Hill to Uddingston cement trains as far as York. The first BR/Sulzer Type 2 (Class 24), D5070, arrived in December 1960 and D5050-72 plus D5094/5 were all allocated by July 1961. By October 1966 they had all left, many migrating to Eastfield or Haymarket. Four Class 10s, D4078/83/4/5, were variously at the depot between November and March 1963.

A classic scene at Finsbury Park as Deltic 55007 *Pinza* stands on number 6 road, with 08551 on the depot's final road beside the water tank. (Brian Morrison)

The depot layout as of 1975. (Alex Fisher)

Finsbury Park

Class 47/4 47421 awaits events outside number 5 road at the depot on March 17, 1979. (Rail-Online)

Initial duties for the depot's fleet included outer London suburban and East Coast Main Line services from King's Cross, freight turns and local shunting diagrams. While the depot did not deal with DMUs, they were stabled in the adjacent Clarence Yard and worked to Cambridge diesel depot for periodic servicing as part of a diagram from King's Cross.

The Deltics arrive

In February 1961 English Electric Type 5 D9001 arrived, the first of the Napier Deltic-powered Express locos for the depot; D9003 was delivered the following month. In June 1961, Finsbury Park received the code 34G and shed plates bearing the designation were affixed to locos. The same month saw the first named Deltic arrive – D9007 *Pinza*. D9001 and D9003 were named *St Paddy* and *Meld* respectively, and by February 1962, D9009 *Alycidon*, D9012 *Crepello*, D9015 *Tulyar*, D9018 *Ballymoss* and D9020 *Nimbus* had arrived direct from Doncaster Works with nameplates already fitted, completing the line-up of racehorse-named Deltics. As the powerful Type 5s arrived, the Class 40s were moved away; D248 went to Gateshead in July 1961 and D201/6/7 went to Stratford, followed in October by D208 and D209.

To mark the cutting in journey time to six hours on the 'Flying Scotsman' service, as well as the centenary of the iconic train, D9020 *Nimbus* had its buffers, couplings and bogies adorned in silver paint along with immaculate bodywork. With the fitting of air brakes to a number of Deltics, some of Haymarket's examples were temporarily transferred to Finsbury Park in order to pool the air-brake examples at the north London depot.

One-offs, prototypes, testing, failures and modifications

Although officially on loan from Brush Traction to Stratford Depot, prototype D0280 *Falcon* spent two weeks at Finsbury Park in October 1961 and had another spell there in April 1962. Between February and June 1962, BR/Sulzer Type 4 (Class 46) D154 was on the depot's books, with D146 between May and June, followed by D155 from June to August. A single BR 0-6-0 shunter (Class 03), D2019, spent November 1963 to May 1964 allocated to the North London facility, followed by a fourth Peak, D174, from April to June 1965. Two more BR/Sulzer Type 2s (Class 25), D7526 and D7600, also spent May 1965 and August to October 1966 at the facility.

In May 1962, Brush Type 2 D5835 was allocated to the depot and was noteworthy for having had its engine up-rated to 2,000hp. It was used on the 0810 King's Cross departure, but left the depot in August 1962. In September 1962, the first Brush Type 4 (Class 47), D1500, arrived, and in the following year a further 27 were allocated, including all 20 'generators' (D1500-19). In September 1963, white-liveried BRCW/Sulzer D0260 *Lion* arrived for testing, and left in February 1964.

The problematic Class 23 English Electric Type 2s spent most of their careers at Finsbury Park. Baby Deltic D5905, recently refurbished and with a new headcode panel to replace the original discs, stands at the fuel point on April 20, 1969. (Rail Photoprints/Dave Cobbe Collection)

THE DIESEL DEPOT | 13

Finsbury Park

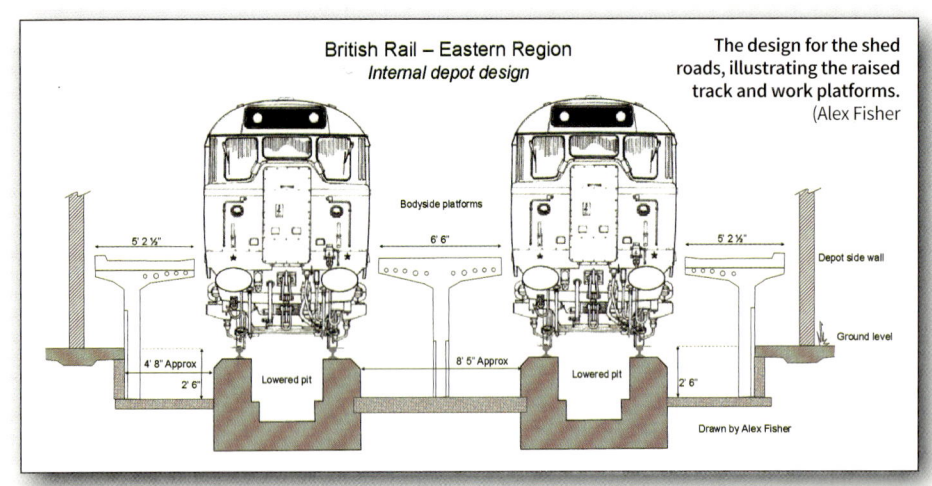

British Rail – Eastern Region
Internal depot design

The design for the shed roads, illustrating the raised track and work platforms.
(Alex Fisher)

Drawn by Alex Fisher

English Electric Type 4 Prototype DP2 was also tested at the depot and arrived in July 1965. It was officially allocated to Finsbury Park from October 1965 until its fateful accident near Thirsk in July 1967.

During a bitterly cold winter of 1962 the Baby Deltics suffered serious engine failures, which led to their withdrawal from traffic and storage. After modifications to the 9-cylinder Napier engines the first loco returned to Finsbury Park from English Electric in mid-1964. The Class 31s were also suffering engine trouble at this time, to the extent that the entire class had to be re-engined with English Electric 1,470hp 12SVT power plants. The first to be dealt with was Finsbury Park's D5677, which was completed in March 1964, and over the following five years the whole class was treated.

The last prototype to be allocated to the depot for a few weeks while it underwent trials on the ECML was Hawker Siddeley's 4,000hp *Kestrel* in October 1969. In late 1972 9009 *Alycidon* was chosen for part experiment DL/381, that saw its No 1 end letter and number headcode box covered over in black film with two 6in white circles allowing light from the first and last digit lamps to shine through. Known as the 'domino' blind, this alteration was later fitted to other BR classes by 1974. To celebrate the Queen's 25-year reign in 1977, 55012 *Crepello* was immaculately turned to work the inaugural 0745 King's Cross to Edinburgh and 1500 return which had especially named 'The Silver Jubilee'.

Disappearing diagrams

The 13 Class 20s (D8020-7 and D8045-9) had all left by April 1966 and of the 103 Brush Type 2s allocated to Finsbury Park between its opening and December 1974, only D5521/33/43/4/89/92/3/6/9/02/4-19/22/23/4/5/6/7/31/33/4/8/9/40/41/2/3/4/5/6/7/8/9/50/51/2/4/76/7/59, and 31108/157/9 remained. The last Baby Deltic (D5909) left in March 1971 and, of the 96 Brush Type 4s resident until December 1974, only D1500-11 were left.

At the end of the 1960s the depot was seeing around 50 locos every 24 hours and in 1973 its code became FP. Although not known for its freight workings, Finsbury Park had a respectable contingent of Class 08 shunters on its books. In February 1978, Hitchin Depot lost its Class 08s (08549/50/57) when they all moved to FP. In 1979 there were nine shunter workings covering two airbraked examples at King's Cross Goods Yard and one each at Ferme Park Reception Sidings, Bounds Green Depot and Finsbury local pilot engine. Three other diagrams covered Welwyn Garden City NCL Depot and two at Hitchin Yard, where one additionally tripped the P-way yard while the other visited Letchworth as required.

Sightings Snapshots

Saturday August 7, 1971

EE Type 4	286
Brush Type 4	1104, 1501/08/11/36/39/49/72/761/64
0-6-0 Shunter	3689/714/717/725
Brush Type 2	5590/94/602/03/04/05/06/11/26/41/43/45/46/47/77/807
EE Type 5	9006/18

Saturday January 20, 1979

Class 08	08553, 08557, 08834
Class 31	31125, 31126, 31192, 31218, 31252, 31407, 31408
Class 46	46043
Class 47	47422
Class 55	55018
Class 15	ADB968002

Saturday March 15, 1980

Class 08	08413, 08810, 08834
Class 31	31225
Class 40	40080
Class 46	46031, 46040, 46041
Class 55	55006

Saturday July 19, 1980

Class 08	08413, 08545, 08551, 08555, 08558, 08709, 08834, 08859
Class 31	31249, 31402, 31407
Class 4	47429, 47523, 47526
Class 55	55009, 55011, 55012, 55015, 55018, 55021

Saturday April 4 1981

Class 08	08551, 08709, 08859
Class 31	31155, 31195, 31218, 31222, 31224, 31225, 31286, 31402, 31403, 31405, 31407, 31408
Class 46	46028, 46044, 46051
Class 47	47162, 47210, 47404, 47428, 47521, 47528
Class 55	55007, 55009, 55013, 55015,

The Class 31 was synonymous with Finsbury Park, with the type used for two decades for empty stock moves, local passenger duties, parcels traffic and freight. Complete with white bodyside stripe, 31403 takes a break between duties on March 17, 1979. (Rail-Online)

Finsbury Park

Wearing its attractive original livery, Brush Type 4 D0280 *Falcon* spent two brief periods at the depot in the early 1960s while undergoing trials on the ECML, and is seen on the fuel roads on October 14, 1961. (Colour-Rail)

Disputes and decline

With the impending introduction of HSTs to the ECML, Finsbury Park was under threat. Angry at the proposed closure, unofficial industrial action was taken by the depot's maintenance staff in the week commencing October 17, 1977. Maintenance staff 'blacked' the Deltic fleet and they were stood down at various depots which resulted in the removal of Deltics from all ECML until the dispute was settled on October 21. During a spell of bad weather in 1979, the maintenance staff were in dispute again and only working on locos allocated to their depot, which led to altered services on the ECML.

In 1978 some of FP's ETH Class 31/4s were painted with a white bodyside stripe, and this was followed on April 6, 1979 with the painting of 55003 *Meld* with distinctive white cab surrounds. Its first outing was on April 7 when it worked 'The Northumbrian' railtour as far as York and return to King's Cross. As depot manager Allan Baker explained to the secretary of state, the cab surrounds were a morale boost to his staff and, surprisingly for the time, the BR board condoned his actions and allowed them to stay. 55015 gained its white cabs on July 12, 1979, followed by 55007/09/18 in August 1979 and 55012 in October. 55001 *St Paddy* and 55020 *Nimbus* were both withdrawn at Doncaster Works at the time and never received white cab surrounds.

To placate the Hull area for not having an HST service, Finsbury Park turned out 55003 *Meld* to work the 'Hull Executive' 1D04 1705 King's Cross to Hull on May 14, 1979 and set a new record for the fastest start-stop time of any BR loco-hauled service – an extraordinary 91.3mph average from King's Cross to Retford.

In 1980 a Deltic damaged the shed doors on No 6 road and another incident saw 47160 roll off the fuel point, through the doors of No 6 road, and into the blocks at the end of the depot. The doors were boarded up and the depot road closed. Finsbury Park ceased to be a maintenance facility on Sunday May 31, 1981 and to commemorate the last Deltic diagram 55009 *Alycidon* carried a headboard on the 1605 King's Cross to York.

There were 50 locos on Finsbury Park's books at the end: ten Class 08s, 24 Class 31s, 12 Class 47s and four Class 55s. The Deltics were 55007, which had been there since June 1961, 55012/15 and 55018. All four had white cab surrounds that were painted out when they were transferred to York.

The December of 1981 was particularly cold and very snowy and the end was near for the Class 55s and, ultimately, Finsbury Park. The last service run of the Deltics was on January 4, 1982 and a few visiting ones were lined up in the adjacent sidings for a final photo call before being towed one or two at a time to Doncaster. The depot continued to provide fuel facilities until October 3, 1983 when Class 47 47408 was the last loco on shed. Upon closure the remaining residents, Class 08s 08558/655/709/813/34/59/73, were all transferred to Bounds Green. After FP's closure it was taken over by the engineer's department for a couple of years, but when they left the shed became vandalised and ultimately bulldozed to make way for valuable housing.

December 1980 and a remarkable line up of six Deltics occupying all shed roads at Finsbury Park. (Colour-Rail/P Zabek)

THE DIESEL DEPOT 15

Tinsley

Of all the new BR depots, perhaps the most effective transformation from steam to diesel was achieved by the Eastern Region (ER) at Tinsley. The Sheffield rationalisation scheme eradicated duplicate yards, and five steam depots were closed and replaced by one yard and the Tinsley Diesel Maintenance Depot (DMD) for the whole of the Sheffield area. The enormity of Tinsley's role can be seen in the way it was designed to maintain around 80 shunting engines and 190 main line locos, covering all of the Sheffield Division, except for those allocated to Wath, Barrow Hill and Shirebrook.

Designing Tinsley Depot

When designing Tinsley, the ER was aware of the shortcomings of Finsbury Park in north London, which had accommodation for three locos per road and thus had a propensity to trap one behind the other. Tinsley therefore employed a double dead end design, with a central workshop and capacity for only two locos per road, meaning six roads on each side of the workshop could hold 12 locos, or 24 in total. It was situated in an elevated position from the rest of Tinsley Yard, with access at either end, although the west end required a zig-zag move in order to gain the required height.

Tinsley's interior design facilitated simultaneous work on three levels. Tracks were supported on short steel columns to allow staff to reach bogie sides at a comfortable height, there were pits for working under locos and a concrete platform 4ft 6in above rail level alongside each berth to give access to the bodyside. Each area of the depot was designated for specific types of work; the four outer roads each had a 1-ton hand-operated crane, while the crane on No 6 road could travel through the workshop area. At the west end of the depot a 5-ton electric crane covered roads 2 to 5. The east end was usually for servicing and minor running repairs, with No 6 east bay for bogie washes and No 2 east for painting. Heavier repairs took place at the west end, such as work on cylinder heads, pistons and turbochargers.

Initially, Tinsley could not undertake engine changes, but could prepare locos for main works visits. On the south side of the shed was an annex building containing two sets of lifting jacks for use during the changing of wheelsets or for bogie swaps. At the rear of the depot there was also a two-stage loco washing plant. The depot's 100,000 gallon fuel stores could be refilled by rail or road. Originally there was a maintenance staffing complement of 200, but retention became a problem as competition for skilled labour came from the many steelworks around Sheffield.

Tinsley from new

Prior to Tinsley's opening, Darnall supplied the majority of the Sheffield Division's diesels with a large allocation of what became Classes 08, 10, 20, 31, 37, 45, 46 and 47. Tinsley was completed in January 1964 and the bulk of Darnall's locos and men were transferred there from April 26, 1964. Tinsley's initial allocation of 160 locos included examples of classes listed above, plus three 'Master and Slave' shunters, which later became Class 13 under TOPS. From June to July 1965, BR/Sulzer Type 2s D5040/6/7/8/9 all had a brief spell based at Tinsley. Darnall retained some shunters, but by October 1965 it

Tinsley

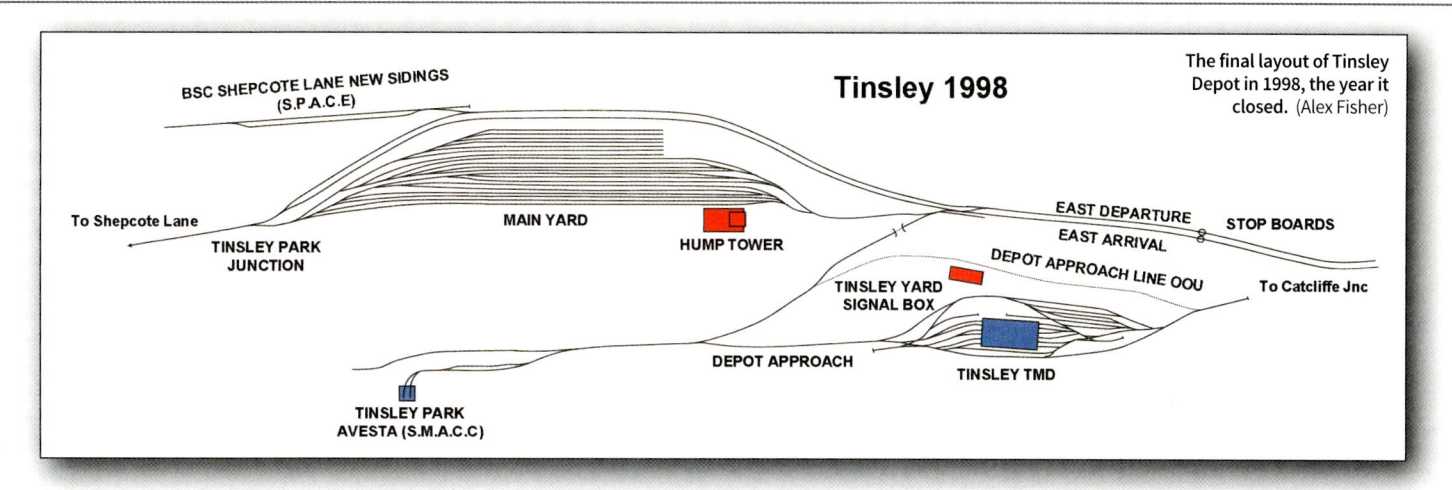

Tinsley 1998

The final layout of Tinsley Depot in 1998, the year it closed. (Alex Fisher)

had lost them to Tinsley, which soon had an incredible 74 on its books. At one point Tinsley had 283 resident locos: Class 08 x 74, 13 x 3, 20 x 12, 17 x 11, 25 x 11, 31 x 57, 37 x 42 and 47/48 x 73.

The Class 13s

Tinsley's three Class 13s were unusual in that they were formed from two previously standard BR 350hp 0-6-0 shunters. As a Master and Slave pairing they were initially coupled back to back, but later nose to tail. D4500, formed of Master unit D4188 and Slave unit D3698, became Class 13 13003. D4501 was Master unit D4190 and Slave unit D4189 which became 13001, while D4502 was Master unit D4187 and Slave unit D3697 became 13002. All were allocated to Tinsley from January 16, 1965.

The units hump shunted Tinsley's yard from opening and two were in use at all times, the third being spare. A generator burn out on the slave unit of 13002 saw it stored from April 9, 1981 and it was withdrawn on June 28; it was the first to be cut up at Swindon Works during October 1982. 13001 and 13003 served until hump shunting ceased in 1984. They were both withdrawn on January 20, 1985 and sent for scrapping at BREL Swindon Works and BREL Doncaster Works respectively.

Declining fortunes

In October 1972 a tranche of Class 25s came to Tinsley along with an ever-growing number of Class 31s. Tinsley's Class 47 allocation was notable for consisting mainly of slow-speed control-fitted examples for MGR coal workings, many of which were out-based at Shirebrook, Barrow Hill and Wath. On March 12, 1984 the miners' strike began and Tinsley soon went from humping 5,000 wagons a week to only 3,000. As the miners' strike continued only 1,500 wagons a week were being humped by November 1984, alongside a further 1,500 that passed through the yard. After the strike ended, colliery closures accelerated and, alongside the diminishing UK steel industry, Tinsley's loco fleet suffered a similar reduction.

Open Days

Like many British Rail depots Tinsley held open days for enthusiasts and local residents, which were also a good way to raise funds for charity. Tinsley's first open day was on June 15, 1980. The event took place

A wintry scene at Tinsley on February 8, 1986 with Classes 20, 31, 37 and 56 all feeling the chill. (Tom Connell)

THE DIESEL DEPOT | 17

Tinsley

LEFT: Inside the maintenance shed in 1965 with two EE Type 1s, an EE Type 3 and a Brush Type 4 D1542 receiving attention. (via Chris Booth)

BELOW LEFT: Class 25 5241 stands among several locos at Tinsley in 1972. At the time it was allocated to the London Midland's Nottingham Division, but was transferred to Tinsley on October 6, 1973 where it became 25091 under TOPS. (Rail-Online)

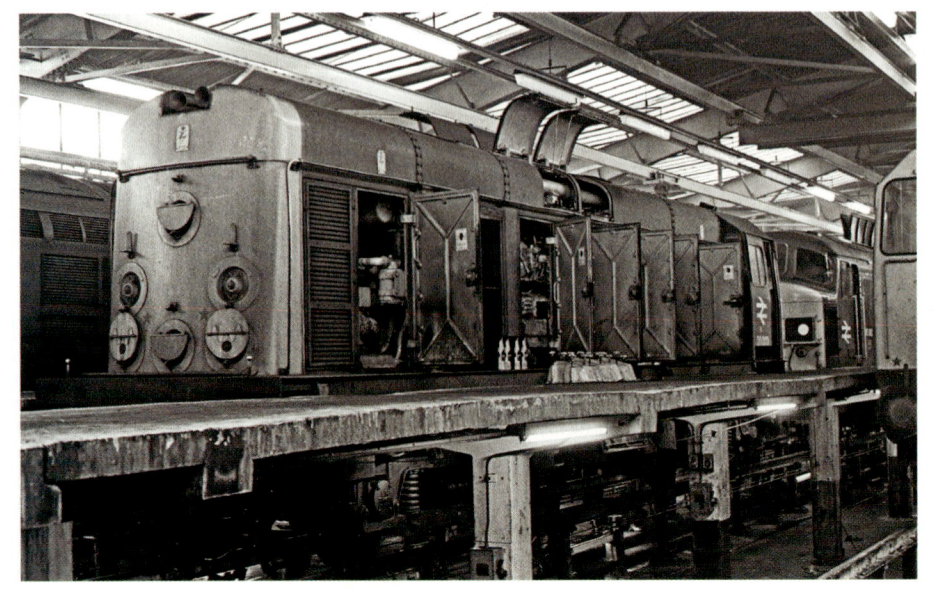

in the servicing shed and attracted more than 25,000 visitors. DMUs were used to shuttle passengers to and from Sheffield Midland Station and a ten-coach railtour entitled 'The White Rose' ran behind Deltic 55018 as the 1Z10 London King's Cross to Sheffield via York. A second railtour was also run by F & W Railtours entitled 'The Tinsley Terror', utilising locomotives 20167, 20174, 37158, 37210, 47267 and 47318 on a route from Newton Abbot through Birmingham to Darnall.

A Family Open Day was held at the TMD on September 20, 1987 but was not open to the general public. Most of the locos on display were all regulars, but a Class 26 was at the depot en route to Vic Berry's Scrapyard in Leicester to be examined for asbestos content along with a Class 58, few of which were ever seen at Tinsley.

To celebrate the depot's Silver Jubilee a third event was held on September 29, 1990. The BRCW Type Three Preservation Group's Railtour 'The Sulzer Rose' used 33042 and 33207 to haul 4-TC sets 8001 and 8014 from Eastleigh to Sheffield; a shuttle service from Sheffield to Tinsley also ran using Metro-Cammell two-car Class 101 DMUs 54056 and 51420 and Class 141s 141016 and 141107.

The final open day on April 27, 1996 saw the committee's expected 10,000 visitors arrive by 1300 and around 11,500 came in total. Hertfordshire Rail Tours 'The Tinsley Humper' ran from King's Cross to Sheffield. Once at Sheffield people had the choice of either visiting the open day or staying on the train for the second part of the rail tour called the 'The Pennine Perambulator'. The charter ran from Sheffield, around Manchester and back, and used a selection of locomotives – 31462, 31468, 37010, 37372 and 47704. Pathfinder Tours also ran the 'Tinsley Open Day Specials' from Westbury to Sheffield with two additional mini tours. The first to Wakefield Kirkgate was behind 59205 and the second to Doncaster behind 59203.

More than 50 locos were on display, the star attractions being six electric locos, 47145 in deep blue with Railfreight Distribution logos, and 47817 making its first public appearance in its new and distinctive Porterbrook livery of white and purple. During the day 08879 was named *Sheffield Children's Hospital* by Richard Jarman from the hospital. More than £40,000 was raised and it was hoped that, after deduction of costs, around £30,000 would go to local charities. Credit for the successful open day was given to Depot Engineer Bill Foster and the open day committee of Phil Hodgkiss, Pete Wylie, Neil Poppleton and Kevin Elliot.

Celebrity locomotives, repaints and private work

In August 1989, two former Southern Region Class 09s (09008 and 09013) came to Tinsley for use on local trip workings. 09013 was later unofficially named *Shepcote* and many other shunters at Tinsley gained names of local places such as *Attercliffe*, *Wath* and *Rotherwood*. In September 1993 both 09s were re-allocated to Cardiff Canton. 09011, 09021 and 09022 came from March to August 1994, whilst 09021 had a second stint at Tinsley from November 1997 until the depot's closure in March 1998.

In the 1990s BR's liveries became ever more diverse and so did Tinsley's embellishments and special repaints. For example, 47145 saw Railfreight Distribution logos applied over a version of BR Blue and when its CEM at Doncaster was cancelled and it received generator repairs at Crewe it retained its special BR Blue livery with black window cab surround and *Merddin Emrys* nameplates. 47375 *Tinsley Traction*

ABOVE: A typical 1970s scene outside the main servicing/maintenance shed with 45025 and 13002 dominating the view. (Rail Photoprints/John Chalcraft)

BELOW: Class 20 20022 with all bonnet doors open during maintenance at Tinsley in 1978. (Michael Rhodes)

Tinsley

ABOVE: Brush Type 2 5801 emerges from the washing plant, which was part of the servicing facilities beside Tinsley Yard, on April 11, 1970. (Rail Photoprints)

Depot was also one of the depot's firm favourites. Originally released into traffic to Immingham depot on December 3, 1965 it was soon allocated to Tinsley, after being loaned to Leeds in 1966 and spending several years at Knottingley. It finally came back to Tinsley in May 1980 where it stayed until the depot's closure. From July 16, 1989, Class 37 37057 came to Tinsley and gained the unofficial name *Viking* on November 12, 1989. After allocations away from Tinsley it came back in 1992 and by early 1993 it was one of just five Class 37s in Large Logo Blue. But Tinsley kept 37057 going along with its unofficial name, until it was placed into an RfD reserve fleet in July 1993.

The RfD Class 47s had their own 'European' livery in which the upper band of the dark grey had been extended further down the body side, and they had a dark blue roof, re-positioned numbers and three light grey Channel Tunnel roundels under the driver's window, all of which helped to give a modern but reserved twist on the Trainload Freight (TLF) triple grey livery. 47217 was the first to receive the new RfD 'European' style livery. It also originally had white TOPS numbers, but as these weren't as visible as black they were soon changed. The first Class 47 to be dealt with for the Freightliner group was 47270, which was released into traffic in early August 1995 sporting the standard triple grey livery but without decals. 47376 was the next loco after it had undergone a light overhaul at ABB Crewe, losing the unofficial *Tinsley Skylark* name when the new Freightliner livery was applied.

With privatisation looming Tinsley began to take on private work, such as Pete Waterman's Class 46 D172 *Ixion* that arrived for an E exam, the work being carried as per the BR specifications and so allowing *Ixion* to return to main line use. In early 1996, Class 50 50044 *Exeter* also visited the depot and although it was the first Class 50 to do so, Tinsley's staff were keen to offer their skills to loco owners and operators.

RfD heyday

As BR's Sectorisation became more entrenched, September 1990 saw 27 Trainload Freight Class

ABOVE: Class 37s 37065 (left) and 37685 inside the maintenance building at Tinsley on October 10, 1987. (Rail Photoprints/Andrew Berry)

BELOW: Master and Slave shunting unit 4502 at Tinsley on July 14, 1973. (Rail-Online)

THE DIESEL DEPOT

Tinsley

Sightings Snapshots

Sunday November 6, 1966 (Clive Greedus)

BR/Sulzer Type 4	D56
Brush Type 4	D1542, D1571, D1574, D1575, D1798, D1865, D1876, D1968, D1868, D1878
0-6-0 Shunter	D3685
Brush Type 2	D5534, D5630, D5681, D5824, D5845
BR/Sulzer Type 2	D7604, D7631, D7633, D7648
EE Type 3	D6710, D6796, D6807, D6810, D6817, D6905, D6803
EE Type 1	D8013, D8014, D8015, D8017, D8018, D8019, D8020, D8058, D8059, D8064, D8065, D8066, D8068, D8069

Saturday March 16, 1974 (RMWeb Vince Minto)

Class 08	3330, 3405, 4045 08024, 08033, 08075, 08218, 08460, 08538, 08801, 08862, 08866, 08878, 08880, Class 13 13001, 13002, 13003
Class 20	8003, 20049, 20058, 20129, 20132, 20208, 20209, 20215
Class 25	5287, 25012, 25016, 25017, 25022, 25078, 25084, 25092, 25150
Class 31	5830, 5834, 31140, 31242, 31300, 31307, 31413
Class 37	37086, 37088, 37101, 37103, 37305
Class 40	356
Class 45	91
Class 46	46021
Class 47	1723, 1753, 1885 47042, 47044, 47053, 47109, 47174, 47297, 47305

Thursday January 18, 1979 (WNXX)

Class 08	08015, 08022, 08024, 08223, 08260, 08266, 08287, 08335, 08485, 08510, 08523, 08861, 08866
Class 13	13001, 13002, 13003
Class 20	20001, 20008, 20010, 20019, 20034, 20056, 20058, 20061, 20098, 20128, 20129
Class 25	25129
Class 31	31142, 31149, 31158, 31175, 31227, 31243, 31263, 31268, 31275, 31302, 31315, 31407
Class 37	37074, 37121, 37226
Class 40	40007
Class 45	45008, 45010, 45016, 45020, 45021, 45022, 45028, 45031, 45035, 45038, 45061
Class 46	46035
Class 47	47044, 47110, 47174, 47177, 47305
Class 56	56002, 56003, 56012, 56014, 56018, 56020, 56022, 56023, 56032

Saturday May 4, 1985 (RMWeb Vince Minto)

Class 08	08244, 08266, 08492, 08507, 08783, 08879, 08880
Class 20	20009, 20025, 20047, 20054, 20055, 20068, 20078, 20086, 20092, 20098, 20105, 20107, 20112, 20116, 20118, 20150, 20162, 20166, 20176
Class 31	31231, 31234, 31237
Class 37	37024, 37030, 37036, 37040, 37130, 37246
Class 45	45066
Class 47	47029, 47147, 47275, 47276, 47379
Class 56	56005, 56013, 56014, 56043, 56093, 56109, 56113

Sunday January 20, 1991 (WNXX)

Class 08	08509, 08749, 08880, 08919,
Class 09	09008, 09013
Class 20	20176, 20198
Class 31	31285, 31405
Class 37	37079, 37110, 37298, 37425
Class 45	45135 (Peak Rail Preserved)
Class 47	47018, 47120, 47145, 47152, 47214, 47220, 47289, 47323, 47332, 47447, 47605

37s re-allocated to other depots as Tinsley headed towards almost exclusive RfD use. The former Buxton out-based Class 37s for aggregate workings went to Immingham, while many of those used by Trainload Steel went to Thornaby. Conversely, RfD brought more of its locos to Tinsley with the transferring of Motherwell-based 37/4 in September 1992. August 1990 saw 18 of Tinsley's Class 47s move into the stored serviceable pools and subsequently some 47/4s went to the Parcels and Provincial Sectors. With the cessation of Speedlink, RfD was prepared to condemn 50 Class 47s, but plans were changed so that they were merely stored or transferred to other sectors short of power. Another change as a result of the Speedlink closures was the disbandment of all Scottish RfD pools except for Eastfield's FDTE fleet of 11 shared Class 37/4, the other 37/0s being dispersed between Tinsley and Thornaby. Tinsley's 37/4 proved useful for summer passenger services from Manchester Victoria to Blackpool North between May and July 1991.

In March 1991, Tinsley's RfD locomotive pools were a main FDAT collection of 110 47/0 and 47/3s with 'all parallel' wiring (which was preferred for longer term use), and 37 Class 47/0 and 47/3s, 'all parallel' but with high engine hours and overdue overhaul, which moved to FDAT pool and were replaced by 23 47/4s. The final FDCT pool held 12 'series parallel' 47/0 and 47/4s that were to be stored at Tinsley to supply parts for FDAT machines before being condemned. On July 8, 1991 Tinsley's active fleet consisted of eight re-geared Class 37s for Manchester Commuter trains and Teesside freight, along with 13 single tank Class 37s for Freightliner traffic in Anglia. December 7, 1992 saw Tinsley's long association with the Class 20 come to an end when 20118, 20137 and 20165 departed for Thornaby. The Class 47s were the most numerous at Tinsley and included 15 for automotive traffic, and 23 twin fuel tank and 104 single tank locos for general use. Tinsley's RfD Class 47s weren't exclusively freight machines, as even in the 1990s they were making appearances on summer Saturday passenger turns such as Birmingham to Yarmouth, Crewe to Holyhead and Blackpool to Liverpool turns, as well as a SX Southport to Manchester Victoria diagram.

The open day on April 27, 1996 was notable for attracting six electric locos, five of which are visible in this image. (Chris booth)

Tinsley

ABOVE: Tinsley's load bank was an old steam tender that had a set of plates inside which, when immersed in a suitable amount of water/brine, created sufficient resistance to load up the generator. The heating produces steam so a close eye always had to be kept on the water level. English Electric Type 3 6866 undergoes load testing on April 11, 1970. (Rail-Online)

In the early 1990s Tinsley's activities were split, as the depot was owned and run by RfD, while the traincrew and local freight work was part of first Trainload Freight and then Loadhaul. On March 13, 1995, Tinsley's 100 drivers and train staff were moved to the train crew depot at Rotherham Steel Terminal. Tinsley was still RfD's heavy maintenance facility at that time and while Loadhaul's Rotherham men shunted the depot, RfD crews from Saltley ferried up to five locos at a time between the depots, as 0Z96 to Saltley and 0J03 to Tinsley.

In October 1995, 30 of Tinsley's Class 47s were transferred to Crewe Diesel Depot for Freightliner's exclusive use, and by March 1996, Tinsley was down to an allocation of 95 Class 47s in three pools. The largest pool was DAET with 74 Class 47s fitted with twin tanks and multiple working equipment, which formed the bulk of the RfD fleet. A single Class 47 could handle a train of up to 1,000 tonnes, but for trains out of Dollands Moor, for example, a pair of Class 47s could handle a train of up to 1,600 tonnes. The paired locomotives were kept together even on lighter duties in order to ensure they stayed on the same diagram and so both would be due for an A exam at 55 TOPS hours at the same time. This greatly aided with planning and diagramming despite not being the best use of the locomotive's assets. On February 24, 1996, EWS bought all of the TLF businesses including the Rotherham Train crew depot and thus most of the workings in and out of the yard, except for any RfD workings and light engines that were visiting Tinsley TMD.

In addition to repair and maintenance, Tinsley undertook several enhancement programmes to its Class 47s, including fitting multiple working equipment, extra fuel tanks and the removal of vacuum exhausters. Most bodywork issues were repairable at Tinsley, 47307 having an entire cab transplant after it was severely damaged by fire. The Tinsley TMD Depot Engineer in 1996 was Bill Foster whose responsibility it was to ensure that at least 56 out of the 76 Class 47s in the DAET pool were available at all times. Tinsley's RfD's work covered a diverse range of duties almost the length and breadth of the British Isles. In the early 1990s locos received light maintenance, and A and B exams at RfD's Dover Town

THE DIESEL DEPOT | 21

Tinsley

Yard fuelling point, Transrail's Cardiff Canton, RES' Crewe Diesel, Mainline's Stratford and Didcot depots and, of course, Saltley. From June 1997, shortly before EWS's purchase of RfD, Virgin Trains Class 47/8 came for contracted repair work.

The end

On March 12, 1997 the Government agreed the sale of RfD to Wisconsin Central, which became EWS. The deal was concluded on November 22, 1997 and it was this move that effectively spelt the end for Tinsley. The EWS and RfD businesses were kept separate for a time but when amalgamation came the closure rumours began almost immediately. Tinsley was a long way from the former RfD West Midlands-centred automotive traffic and, as EWS had depots available at Bescot, Saltley, Crewe and Toton, by late 1997 EWS confirmed its intention to close Tinsley. Staff were offered redundancy or the opportunity to transfer to other depots.

At the end of February 1998, 13 scrap Class 47s were cleared from the depot, with 37242 hauling away the last

RIGHT: Class 56 56099 stands amid the snow outside the maintenance shed on February 8, 1986. (Tom Connell)

BELOW: Depending on your viewpoint this was either colourful or dreadful. Porterbrook showing off its purple and white colour scheme on 47817 at the open day on April 27, 1996. (Chris Booth)

22 THE DIESEL DEPOT

Tinsley

LEFT: Four RfD Class 47s, including 47314, are flanked by two Class 37s in the maintenance shed on May 9, 1993. (Colour-Rail/D Pye)

BELOW: Class 08 08879 was named *Sheffield Children's Hospital* at the 1996 open day on April 27. The loco is currently stored at Eastleigh Works.
(Chris Booth)

reign as an active depot to an end, and 08879 was re-allocated to Doncaster upon closure.

With the once great depot now silent, a gathering at the Railway Club, Sheffield, was held on April 4, 1998 to mark its end. Vandals and thieves soon attacked the infrastructure meaning demolition was rapid, which thwarted any potential buyer or further lease of life. The site was completely cleared by June 2006 and the land sold for redevelopment as a hotel and car dealership. Today it is no more, although there is a small collection of sidings aside a large distribution building that occupies a sizable part of the former marshalling yard.

two (47543 and 475200). On March 5, 1998, 47218 and 47147 entered the depot for C exams and were the very last locos to receive attention at Tinsley. Officially, RfD Class 47 maintenance continued up to March 13 when the remaining examples were all re-allocated to Saltley. Tinsley's final Class 08s included 08535/905/46/51 and 09011 out-based at Saltley, while 08413 and 08751 were stored at the depot and only 08879 was operational.

On March 27, 1998, 47145 *Merddin Emrys* was the final locomotive on shed. 47375 *Tinsley Traction Depot* arrived from Saltley to collect it and the two Class 47s were positioned alongside 08879 *Sheffield Children's Hospital* for a final photo call. When the 47s departed as 0Z96 1500, Tinsley to Saltley, they brought Tinsley's

Master and Slave hump shunter 13001 with the vast marshalling yard behind and the servicing depot to the right in May 1983.
(Colour-Rail/T B Owen)

THE DIESEL DEPOT | 23

Depot Heydays 1968-1983

24 | THE DIESEL DEPOT

www.railwaysillustrated.co.uk

Depot Heydays 1968-1983

The post-steam era was a fairly stable, if declining, environment for BR's diesel depots. The industry recognised that it would need to keep its depot requirement under review due to changing traffic patterns and modes of operation. The adjacent table shows a 1965 view of what BR visualised the composition of its diesel depot to be upon the eradication of steam.

LEFT: Shirebrook Depot on July 11, 1984 during the miners' strike. Considerable numbers of Tinsley-based Class 56s dominated the depot and even spilled along the line to Warsop Main colliery, where 56030, 56115, 56008, 56113 and 56098 are parked. The subsequent run-down of the coal industry had a severe impact on depots such as this. (Michael Rhodes)

BELOW: Westhouses Depot in Derbyshire is a good example of a facility that soldiered on whatever happened. This view was taken on November 23, 1969 before the old steam shed roof was removed. For several years into the 1980s the walls remained and the depot continued to act as a stabling point for coal traffic locos. (Rail Photoprints/Hugh Ballantyne)

Expected Diesel Depots

Region	Maintenance	Servicing
Eastern	10	9
London Midland	21	14
North Eastern	10	-
Scottish	15	3
Southern	7	4
Western	9	16
Total	72	46

Depots and allocations

An issue that came to the fore in 1965 was whether it was better to allocate locos to individual depots for all their maintenance or place them in a common user pool to receive attention at whichever depot was most convenient. Although unsanctioned by BR's HQ engineering staff, from January 16, 1965 the LMR took the bold decision to base some of its locos under a new system of four divisions: D14 London Midland, D15 Leicester Division and D16 Nottingham Division; the remainder were simply allocated to the Midland Line (ML). The system seemed to have its merits for it allowed for a more even distribution of work among the region's depots, and a check in late 1966/early 1967 revealed that of the 140 diesels affected by the change, only two were found to be overdue for minor maintenance – a performance hard to beat under any system. The counter argument to the common user approach was that the dedication of locos to specific depots fostered a greater sense of ownership and responsibility by a depot's staff and management, as seen with Finsbury Park's Deltics and later Tinsley, with its named Class 47s and custom repaints.

The ER and North Eastern Region (NER) were merged in late 1966 and when Knottingley Depot opened in 1967, the standard ER design wasn't perpetuated, although it was very similar in many respects. Its purpose was to supply freight locos, mainly slow-speed fitted Class 47/3s for Merry-go-Round (MGR) coal services between the local collieries and power stations.

One of the last large new depots to open was Eastfield, which was rebuilt at the end of the 1960s and opened in 1971. The time was perhaps the high water mark for

Depot Heydays 1968-1983

For years Bristol Bath Road had the largest loco allocation on the WR, some of which are shown in this 1978 image, but the arrival of the HST and the demise of much freight in the area gradually saw it lose its importance and eventually close in September 1995. (Michael Rhodes)

Britain's diesel depots. Many small outposts retained an allocation of a shunter or two, such as Burton upon Trent with four in October 1971, while the likes of Crewe Diesel Depot with 40 Class 08s and a further 172 main line types represented the large depot at its best.

Scotland's major depots were Eastfield, which had 19 shunters and 110 main line locos, and Haymarket which had five shunters and 130 main line engines, including eight Deltics. Polmadie with 88 engines and Inverness with 39 also had significant numbers.

On the Southern, Eastleigh had 92 engines on its books in August 1971 and Hither Green had 66, while Stewarts Lane had electro-diesels E6001-49. In addition, many of the EMU depots usually had a few Class 08s allocated, and Selhurst with 27 shunters was the largest. The

Depot numbers and codes

London Midland

1 Willesden

Code	Dates	Abbr	Name
1A	1950-1973	WN	Willesden
1B	1950-1966	CM	Camden
1C	1950-1965	WJ	Watford
1D	1950-1963		Devons Road, Bow, became 1J
	1963-1973	ME	Marylebone station, previously 14F
1E	1952-1973	BY	Bletchley
Sub-sheds		AL	Aylesbury (to 1962)
		CA	Cambridge
			Leighton Buzzard (to 1962)
			Newport Pagnell (to 1955)
1F	1963-1968	RU	Rugby, previously 2A
1G	1963-1965		Woodford Halse, previously 2F
1H	1963-1965	NN	Northampton, previously 2E
1J	1963-1964		Devons Road, Bow, previously 1D

2 Rugby

Code	Dates	Abbr	Name
2A	1950-1963	RU	Rugby, became 1F
Sub-sheds			Market Harborough (to 1955)
			Seaton (to 1960)
	1963-1973	TS	Tyseley, previously 84E
2B	1950-1950	BY	Bletchley, became 4A
	1950-1963		Nuneaton, previously 2D, became 5E 1963-1968
	1963-1968		Wolverhampton Oxley
2C	1950-1950	NN	Northampton, became 4B
	1950-1958		Warwick (Milverton), previously 2E
	1963-1967		Stourbridge Jn, previously 84F
2D	1950-1950		Nuneaton, became 2B
	1950-1958		Coventry, previously 2F
	1963-1966		Banbury, previously 84C
2E	1950-1950		Warwick (Milverton), became 2C
	1952-1963	NN	Northampton, became 1H
Sub-shed			Blisworth, previously 4B
	1963-1973	SY	Saltley
2F	1950-1950		Coventry, became 2D
	1955-1958		Market Harborough, became 15F
	1958-1963		Woodford Halse, previously 2G, became 1G
	1963-1973	BS	Bescot, previously 21B
2G	1958-1958		Woodford Halse, previously 38E, became 2F
	1963-1967		Rycroft, Walsall, previously 21F
2H	1963-1967		Monument Lane, previously 21E
2J	1963-1965		Aston, previously 21D
2K	1963-1965		Wolverhampton Bushbury, previously 21C
2L	1963-1965		Leamington Spa, previously 84D
2M	1963-1964		Wellington (Salop), previously 84H

Code	Dates	Abbr	Name
2P	1963-1964		Kidderminster, previously 84G

3 Bescot

Code	Dates	Abbr	Name
3A	1950-1960	BS	Bescot, became 21B
3B	1950-1960		Bushbury, became 21C
3C	1950-1960		Rycroft, became 21F
3D	1950-1960		Aston, became 21D
3E	1950-1960		Monument Lane, became 21E
Sub-sheds			Albion
			Tipton

4 Bletchley (until 1952)

Code	Dates	Abbr	Name
4A	1950-1952	BY	Bletchley
Sub-sheds			Aylesbury
		CA	Cambridge
			Leighton Buzzard
			Newport Pagnell
			Oxford (1950), previously 2B, became 1E
4B	1950-1952	NN	Northampton
Sub-shed			Blisworth, previously 2C, became 2E

5 Stoke Division (D05)

Code	Dates	Abbr	Name
5A	1950-1965		Crewe North
	1965-1973	CE/CD	Crewe Diesel Depot
5B	1950-1967		Crewe South
5C	1950-1965		Stafford
5D	1950-1967		Stoke
5E	1950-1962		Alsager
	1963-1966		Nuneaton, previously 2B
5F	1950-1966		Uttoxeter
5H	1963-1965		WCML electric loco fleet Code ACL used 1960-1963 and from 1966

6 Chester

Code	Dates	Abbr	Name
6A	1950-1973		Chester (Midland)
6B	1950-1966		Mold Jn
6C	1950-1963	BC	Birkenhead Mollington Street, became 8H
	1963-1967		Croes Newydd, previously 89B
Sub-sheds			Bala (to 1965)
			Penmaenpool (to 1965)
6D	1950-1960		Chester (Northgate)
	1963-1967		Shrewsbury, previously 89A
6E	1950-1958		Wrexham Rhosddu, became 84K
	1958-1960		Chester (WR), previously 84K
	1963-1965		Oswestry, previously 89D
6F	1950-1963		Bidston
	1963-1966		Machynlleth, previously 89C
Sub-sheds			Aberystwyth (to 1965)
			Pwllheli (to 1966)
	1967-1973	VR	Aberystwyth VoR
6G	1952-1966		Llandudno Jn, previously 7A
6H	1952-1965		Bangor, previously 7B

Code	Dates	Abbr	Name
6J	1952-1967	HD	Holyhead, previously 7C 6K 1952-1963 Rhyl
Sub-shed			Denbigh (to 1955), previously 7D

7 Llandudno Jn (until 1952)

Code	Dates	Abbr	Name
7A	1950-1952	LJ	Llandudno Jn, became 6G
7B	1950-1952		Bangor, became 6H
7C	1950-1952	HD	Holyhead, became 6J
7D	1950-1952		Rhyl
Sub-shed			Debigh, became 6K

8 Liverpool Edge Hill

Code	Dates	Abbr	Name
8A	1950-1968	EG	Edge Hill (Liverpool), became sub-shed of 8J
8B	1950-1967		Warrington (Dallam)
Sub-shed		WA	Warrington (Arpley) (to 1963)
8C	1950-1968		Speke Jn
8D	1950-1964		Widnes, previously sub-shed of 13E
8E	1950-1958		Brunswick (Liverpool), previously 13E, became 27F
	1958-1968		Northwich, previously 9G
8F	1958-1973	SP	Springs Branch (Wigan)
Sub-shed			Sutton Oak (1967-1969), previously 10A
8G	1950-1967		Sutton Oak, became sub-shed of 8F
8H	1960-1963	AN	Allerton, became 8J
	1963-1967	BC	Birkenhead Mollington Street, previously 6C
8J	1963-1973	AN	Allerton, previously 8H
8K	1963-1966		Bank Hall, previously 27A
8L	1963-1967		Aintree, previously 27B
8M	1963-1967		Southport, previously 27C
8P	1963-1964		Wigan Central, previously 27D
8R	1963-1963		Walton, previously 27E

9 Manchester Longsight

Code	Dates	Abbr	Name
9A	1950-1973	LO	Longsight (Manchester)
9B	1950-1968	SQ	Stockport (Edgeley)
9C	1958-1961		Macclesfield
Sub-shed		RS	Reddish (1958-1963), previously sub-shed of 39A
	1963-1973	RS	Reddish
Sub-shed			Dinting, previously sub-shed of 39A
9D	1950-1963	BX	Buxton, became 9L
	1963-1973	NH	Newton Heath, previously 26A
9E	1950-1968	TP	Trafford Park (Manchester), previously 13A, coded 17F 1957-58
9F	1950-1968		Heaton Mersey, previously 13C, coded 17E 1957-58
9G	1950-1958	NW	Northwich, previously 13D, became 8E
	1958-1965		Gorton, previously 9H
Sub-shed		RS	Reddish (1958-1963)
9H	1958-1958		Gorton
Sub-shed			Dinting (1958), previously 39A, became 9G
9J	1963-1966		Agecroft, previously 26B
9K	1963-1968		Bolton, previously 26C
9L	1963-1968	BX	Buxton, previously 9D

26 THE DIESEL DEPOT

Depot Heydays 1968-1983

biggest depot on the Western Region was Bristol Bath Road that had 22 shunters and 94 main line engines in October 1971.

In July 1975 six major depots accounted for 1,128 locos. Toton with 282 was the largest, followed by Eastfield (220), Tinsley (200), Cardiff (168), Gateshead (143) and Stratford (115). Despite falling freight volumes and an ever-greater move towards DMUs and later HSTs, relatively few diesel depots closed during the 1970s. The few that did were those that had clung on mainly as a traincrew depot with stabling facilities, such as Kirkby-in-Ashfield and Colwick in Nottinghamshire. Both had enjoyed large steam allocations and Kirkby even had a brief liaison with diesels in the form of Peak D94 in the last quarter of 1964, most likely for crew training. Its steam locos had been steadily withdrawn or transferred away until, in February 1967, only BR 0-6-0 shunter D3696 remained, although it moved to Burton on October 14, 1967. Diesels were still stabled at Kirkby until November 11, 1970, but after that they used Westhouses, Shirebrook or Toton.

Traincrew and loco depots are often thought of as one and the same, but at Burton for example, the train crew depot closed in 1975 and while most of the staff relocated to Coalville, the locos only stabled there, returning to Burton for fuel. There were many examples of depots without crew and crew depots without stabling facilities, let alone allocations. To illustrate this, after the closure of Westhouses Depot a loco convoy of two Class 20s

Gloucester Hornton Road was not a particularly significant facility, with only shunters based there and being used primarily for servicing and stabling. However, it did continue to see use into the privatisation era. On August 8, 1979 PWM650 shares the depot with 08826 and 37206. (Rail Photoprints/Gordon Edgar)

and three Class 58s was ferried from Toton to Tibshelf Sidings on a Monday morning for use by Westhouses' train crews. They were swapped throughout the week for fuelled examples until they all returned to Toton for weekend stabling. Worksop and Barrow Hill were two other depots that also sent engines further afield for fuel and servicing, with Tinsley, Shirebrook and Toton all being visited as required.

Sub-sheds			Cromford (1963-1967)
			Middleton Top (1963-1967)
			Sheep Pasture (1963-1967)
9M	1963-1965	BQ	Bury, previously 26D
9P	1963-1964		Lees (Oldham), previously 26E

10 Wigan (until 1958) Carnforth (from 1963)

10A	1950-1958	SP	Springs Branch (Wigan), became 8F
	1963-1968		Carnforth, previously 24L
10B	1950-1958	PS	Preston, became 24K
	1963-1964		Blackpool Central
Sub-shed		BP	Blackpool North, previously 28A, became sub-shed of 10C
10C	1950-1958		Patricroft, became 26F 1963-1968 Fleetwood, previously 28B
10D	1950-1954		Plodder Lane
	1955-1958		Sutton Oak, previously 10E, became 8G
	1963-1972	LH	Lostock Hall (Preston), previously 24C
10E	1950-1955		Sutton Oak, became 10D
10F	1950-1952		Lower Ince, Wigan, previously 13G
	1963-1968		Rose Grove, previously 24B
10G	1963-1967		Skipton, previously 23A
10H	1963-1967		Lower Darwen, previously 24D
10J	1963-1966		Lancaster (Green Ayre), previously 24J

11 Carnforth / Barrow

11A	1950-1958		Carnforth, became 24L
	1958-1960	BW	Barrow-in-Furness, previously 11B, became 12E
11B	1950-1958	BW	Barrow-in-Furness, became 11A
	1958-1969		Workington, previously 12C, became 12F
11C	1950-1960		Oxenholme, became 12G
11D	1950-1960		Tebay, became 12H
11E	1951-1957		Lancaster (Green Ayre), previously 23C, became 24J

12 Carlisle

12A	1950-1958	CL	Carlisle (Upperby), became 12B
	1958-1973		Carlisle (Kingmoor)
Sub-shed			Durran Hill (to 1959), previously 68A
12B	1950-1950	CL	Carlisle (Upperby), became 12A
	1950-1951		Carlisle (Canal), became 68E
	1955-1955		Penrith, previously 12C, reopened as sub-shed 1958
	1958-1968		Carlisle (Upperby)
Sub-shed			Penrith (1958-1962), previously 12A
12C	1950-1955		Penrith
Sub-shed			Silloth (to 1953), became 12B
	1955-1958		Workington, previously 12D, became 11B
	1958-1963		Carlisle (Canal), previously 12D, became 12C
	1963-1977		Barrow-in-Furness, previously 12E
12D	1950-1955		Workington, became 12C
	1958-1958		Carlisle (Canal), previously 68E, became 12C

	1958-1961		Kirkby Stephen, previously 12E
	1963-1968		Workington, previously 12F
12E	1950-1954		Moor Row
	1958-1958		Kirkby Stephen, previously 51H, became 12D
	1960-1963		Barrow-in-Furness, previously 11, became 12C
	1963-1968		Tebay, previously 12H

13 Manchester Trafford Park (until 22 May 1950)

13A	1950-1950		Trafford Park, became 9E 13B 1950-1950 Belle Vue
Sub-shed			Gowhole, became 26G
13C	1950-1950		Heaton Mersey, became 9F 13D
	1950-1950		Northwich, became 9G
13E	1950-1950		Brunswick (Liverpool)
Sub-shed			Widnes, became 8E
13F	1950-1950		Walton, became 27E
13G	1950-1950		Lower Ince, Wigan, became 10F

14 Cricklewood

14A	1950-1963	CD	Cricklewood, became Cricklewood West (14B)
	1963-1973	CD/CW	Cricklewood East
14B	1950-1963		Kentish Town
	1963-1967		Cricklewood West, previously Cricklewood (14A)
14C	1950-1960		St Albans 1963-1971 Bedford, previously 14E
14D	1950-1962		Neasden
Sub-shed			Maryleybone station (to 1961)
14E	1958-1963	BE	Bedford, previously 15D, became 14C
14F	1961-1963		Marylebone, previously sub-shed of 14D, became 1D

15 Wellingborough

15A	1950-1968	WO	Wellingborough
Sub-shed			Market Harborough (1963-1965), became 15B
	1963-1973	LR	Leicester (Midland), previously 15C
15B	1950-1963		Kettering, became 15C
	1963-1973	WO	Wellingborough, previously 15A
15C	1950-1963	LR	Leicester (Midland)
Sub-shed			Market Harborough (from 1960), became 15A
	1963-1965		Kettering, previously 15B
15D	1950-1958	BE	Bedford, became 14E
	1950-1963	CV	Coalville, previously 17C, became 15E
	1963-1964		Leicester (Great Central), previously 15E
15E	1958-1963		Leicester (Great Central), previously 38C, became 15D
	1963-1965	CV	Coalville, previously 15D
15F	1958-1960		Market Harborough, previously 2F, became sub-shed of 15C

16 Nottingham (until 1963) Toton (from 1963)

16A	1950-1963		Nottingham (Midland)
Sub-sheds			Lincoln St Marks (to 1953)
			Southwell (to 1955), became 16D

	1963-1973	TO	Toton, previously 18A
16B	1950-1950		Peterborough (Spital Bridge), became 35C
	1955-1963		Kirkby-in-Ashfield, previously 16C, became 16E
	1963-1966		Annesley, previously 16D
	1966-1970		Colwick, previously 40E
16C	1950-1955		Kirkby-in-Ashfield, became 16B
	1955-1960		Mansfield, previously 16D
	1963-1973	DY	Derby
Sub-shed			Rowsley (1964-1967), previously 17A
16D	1950-1955		Mansfield, became 16C
	1958-1963		Annesley, previously 38B, became 16B
	1963-1967		Nottingham, previously 16A
16E	1963-1966		Kirkby-in-Ashfield, previously 16B
16F	1963-1973	BU	Burton-on-Trent, previously 17B
16G	1963-1966	WU	Westhouses, previously 18B, post 1975, became WT
16H	1963-1964		Hasland
Sub-sheds			Chesterfield (1963)
			Clay Cross Works (1963)
			Morton Colliery (1963)
			Williamsthorpe Colliery, previously 18C
16J	1963-1964		Rowsley, previously 17C, became sub-shed of 16C

17 Derby (until 9 September 1963)

17A	1950-1963	DY	Derby, became 16C
17B	1950-1963	BU	Burton-upon-Trent
Sub-sheds			Horninglow (to 1960)
			Overseal, became 16F
17C	1950-1958	CV	Coalville, became 15D
	1958-1963		Rowsley
Sub-sheds			Cromford (to 1960)
			Middleton Top
			Sheep Pasture, previously 17D, became 16J
17D	1950-1958		Rowsley
Sub-sheds			Cromford
			Middleton Top
			Sheep Pasture
17E	1957-1958		Heaton Mersey Code 9F to January 1957 and from April 1958 17F 1957-1958
			Trafford Park Code 9E to January 1957 and from April 1958

18 Toton (until 9 September 1963)

18A	1950-1963	TO	Toton, became 16A
18B	1950-1963	WU	Westhouses, became 16G, post 1975, became WT
18C	1950-1963		Hasland, became 16H
Sub-sheds			Chesterfield
			Clay Cross Works
			Morton Colliery
			Williamsthorpe Colliery

THE DIESEL DEPOT 27

Depot Heydays 1968-1983

A good example of how long some steam-era infrastructure lasted is the coal stage at Immingham – still in-situ on May 11, 1985. Stabled nearby were 37069, 47299, 47295, 47105, 47358 and 47222. (Rail Photoprints/Gordon Edgar)

stayed relatively the same year after year and although some classes were withdrawn and working practices slowly modernised, it wasn't until 1981 that major changes were afoot.

In October 1981 the Railway Executive Group met to discuss a strategic plan for depot rationalisation. The group envisaged the closure of five Traction Maintenance Depots and a further four reduced in status, along with doing away with 20 fuelling and servicing points. However, the group also recognised that it might be prudent to build a small number of new maintenance and/or servicing depots owing to the changing pattern of both civil engineering requirements and selected bulk movements such as coal.

The philosophy of the minimum number of TMDs was the objective, without regard to regional boundaries in relation to maintenance and train crew facilities. On Sunday May 31, 1981 Finsbury Park ceased work as a maintenance centre and its 40 main line locos were transferred away, leaving just ten Class 08s. The move was forecast to save BR £600,000 per annum. Fuel facilities remained until October 3, 1983 when the depot closed and its final seven Class 08s were transferred to Bounds Green. In January 1982, York was also to be reduced in status to a fuelling and inspection point at an annual saving of £310,000, while the unions had been informed of the intention to reduce Thornaby's status. Of the 20 Fuel and Inspection Point (FIP) closures, Ranelagh Bridge (Paddington), Workington,

Reaching a peak

By 1980 there had been few depots closures and as of December 31, 1980 there was a total of 78 depots of all types, along with 51 fuel and inspection points. These figures were actually slightly higher than in 1965 and aside from a few openings and closures, there had been few changes. The era of BR blue was characterised as one of monotony and stability. A depot's allocation

18D	1950-1958	BH	Barrow Hill (Staveley)
Sub-sheds			Sheepbridge
			Staveley New Works
			Staveley Old Works, became 41E
19 Sheffield (until 1 February 1958)			
19A	1950-1958		Sheffield Grimesthorpe, became 41B
19B	1950-1958		Millhouses (Sheffield), became 41C
19C	1950-1958		Canklow, became 41D
20 Leeds (until 3 February 1957)			
20A	1950-1957	HO	Leeds (Holbeck), became 55A
20B	1950-1957		Leeds (Stourton), became 55B
20C	1950-1957		Royston, became 55D
20D	1950-1957		Normanton, became 55E 20E
	1950-1957		Bradford (Manningham)
Sub-shed			Ilkley, became 55F 20F
	1950-1950		Skipton
Sub-shed			Keighley Code 23A 26 June 1950 to 7 October 1951, became 24G
20G	1950-1957		Hellifield Code 23B 26 June 1950 to 7 October 1951, became 24H
20H	1950-1950		Lancaster (Green Ayre), became 23C
21 Saltley (until 9 September 1963)			
21A	1950-1963	SY	Saltley (Birmingham), became 2C
Sub-sheds			Camp Hill
			Kingsbury
			Water Orton
			Stratford-upon-Avon (1953-1962)
21B	1950-1960		Bourneville
Sub-shed			Redditch
21C	1950-1958		Bromsgrove, became 85F
	1960-1963		Bushbury, previously 3B, became 2K
21D	1950-1953		Stratford-upon-Avon
Sub-shed			Blisworth (to 7 July 1950), became sub-shed of 21A
	1950-1973		Aston, previously 3D, became 2J
21E	1960-1963		Monument Lane, previously 3E, became 2H
21F	1950-1963		Ryecroft (Walsall), previously 3C, became 2G
22 Bristol (until 1 February 1958)			
22A	1950-1958		Bristol (Barrow Road), became 82E
22B	1950-1958	GL	Gloucester (Barnwood)
Sub-sheds			Dursley, Tewkesbury, became 85E
23 Liverpool Bank Hall (until 10 June 1950) Skipton (24 June 1950 to 7 October 1951)			
23A	1950-1950		Liverpool (Bank Hall), became 27A
	1950-1951		Skipton Code 20F until 24 June 1950 and from 7 October 1951
23B	1950-1950		Aintree, became 27B 1950-1951 Hellifield Code 20G until 24 June 1950 and from 7 October 1951
23C	1950-1950		Southport, became 27C
	1950-1951		Lancaster (Ayre Green) Code 20H until 24 June 1950 and from 7 October 1951

23D	1950-1950		Wigan (L&Y), became 27D
24 Accrington (until 9 September 1963)			
24A	1950-1963		Accrington, became 10E
24B	1950-1963		Rose Grove, became 10F
24C	1950-1963		Lostock Hall, became 10D
24D	1950-1963		Lower Darwen, became 10H
24E	1950-1963		Blackpool Central Code 28A 10 June 1960 to 1 April 1952, became 10B
Sub-shed			Blackpool North
24F	1950-1963		Fleetwood Code 28B 10 June 1960 to 1 April 1952, became 10C
24G	1957-1963		Skipton, previously 20F, became 10G
24H	1957-1963		Hellifield, previously 20G
24J	1957-1963		Lancaster (Green Ayre), previously 11E, became 10J
24K	1958-1961		Preston, previously 10B
24L	1958-1963		Carnforth, previously 11A, became 10A
25 Wakefield (until September 1956)			
25A	1950-1956		Wakefield, became 56A
25B	1950-1957		Huddersfield, became 55G
25C	1950-1956		Goole, became 53E
25D	1950-1956		Mirfield, became 56D
25E	1950-1956		Sowerby Bridge, became 56E
25F	1950-1956		Low Moor, became 56F
25G	1950-1956		Farnley Jn, became 55C
26 Newton Heath (until 9 September 1963)			
26A	1950-1963		Newton Heath, became 9D
26B	1950-1963		Agecroft, became 9J
26C	1950-1963		Bolton, became 9K
26D	1950-1963	BQ	Bury, became 9M
26E	1950-1954		Bacup
	1955-1963		Lees (Oldham), previously 26F, became 9P
26F	1950-1955		Lees (Oldham), became 26E
	1955-1956		Belle Vue (Manchester), previously 13B, became 26G
	1958-1963		Patricroft, previously 10C, became 9H
26G	1950-1955		Belle Vue (Manchester), previously 13B, became 26F
27 Liverpool Bank Hall (10 June 1950 to 9 September 1963)			
27A	1950-1963		Liverpool (Bank Hall), previously 23A, became 8K
27B	1950-1963		Aintree, previously 23B, became 8L
27C	1950-1963		Southport, previously 23C, became 8M
27D	1950-1963		Wigan (L&Y), previously 23D, became 8P
27E	1950-1963		Walton, previously 13F, became 8R
27F	1950-1961		Brunswick (Liverpool), previously 8E
28 Blackpool (10 June 1950 to 1 April 1952)			
28A	1950-1952		Blackpool Central
Sub-shed			Blackpool North Code 24E until 10 June 1950 and from 1 April 1952

28B	1950-1952		Fleetwood Code 24F until 10 June 1950 and from 1 April 1952
Eastern Region			
30 Stratford			
30A	1950-1973	SX/SF	Stratford
Sub-sheds			Bishops Stortford (1959-1960)
			Brentwood (to 1957)
			Canning Town
			Chelmsford
		CC/CL	Clacton (1959-1963)
		CR	Colchester (1967-1968)
			Enfield (to 1960)
			Epping (to 1957)
			Hertford East (1960)
			Ilford
			Palace Gates (to 1954)
			Spitalfields
			Ware
			Wood Street
			Temple Mills (to 1964)
			Walton-on-the-Naze (1959-1963)
30B	1950-1960		Hertford East, became sub-shed of 30A
Sub-sheds			Buntingford (to 1959)
30C	1950-1959		Bishops Stortford, became sub-shed of 30A in 1959
30D	1950-1956		Southend (Victoria), became sub-shed of 30A
30E	1950-1959	CR	Colchester Reopened as sub-shed of 30A 1967
Sub-sheds			Braintree
			Clacton
			Kelevedon (to 1951)
			Maldon
			Walton-on-the-Naze
	1968-1973	CR	Colchester
30F	1950-1967		Parkeston Quay
31 Cambridge			
31A	1950-1973	CA	Cambridge
Sub-sheds			Ely
			Huntingdon East (to .1961)
			Saffron Walden (to 1958)
			Thaxted (to 1952)
31B	1950-1973		March
Sub-sheds		MC/MR	King's Lynn (1960-1962)
			South Lynn (1960-c1961)
			Wisbech (1952-?)
31C	1950-1960		King's Lynn, became sub-shed of 31B
Sub-sheds			Hunstanton (to 1958)
			South Lynn (1959-1960)
			Wisbech (to 1952)

Depot Heydays 1968-1983

Newport Ebbw Junction in 1977 with four Class 08s and a Class 37 on shed. It closed five years later in October 1982. (Michael Rhodes)

Fort William, Burton, Newton Abbot, Tyne Yard and Wellingborough all took place in 1981. 1982 included some drastic proposals, with the TMDs at March and Wigan both proposed for closure, along with reducing Margam's status to a FIP and closing the FIPs at Newport Ebbw Junction, Ferryhill (Aberdeen), Grangemouth, Dunfermline Townhill, Holbeck, Barrow Hill, Edge Hill and Westhouses. The following year saw Manchester Longsight closed, with the FIPs at Saltley or Bescot under threat along with Holbeck, Margam, Wath, Cambridge Street, Millerhill, Northwich and Gloucester. Looking longer term, there were also plans to reduce one depot

31D	1950-1959		South Lynn, became sub-shed of 31C
31E	1950-1959		Bury St Edmunds
Sub-shed			Sudbury
31F	1958-1960		Peterborough Spital Bridge, previously 35C
32 Norwich			
32A	1950-1973	NO/NR	Norwich
Sub-sheds			Cromer High (to 1954)
			Dereham (to 1955)
			Swaffham
			Wells (to 1963)
			Wymondham
			Yarmouth South Town (1959-1962)
32B	1950-1968		Ipswich
Sub-sheds			Aldeburgh (to 1956)
			Felixstowe (to 1959)
			Framlingham (to 1952)
			Laxfield (to 1952)
			Stowmarket
32C	1950-1962		Lowestoft
32D	1950-1959		Yarmouth South Town, became sub-shed of 32A
32E	1950-1959		Yarmouth (Vauxhall)
32F	1950-1959		Yarmouth Beach
32G	1950-1959		Melton Constable
Sub-sheds			Cromer Beach, Norwich City
33 Plaistow			
33A	1950-1959		Plaistow
Sub-sheds			Upminster (to 1956), became sub-shed of 33B in 1959
33B	1950-1962		Tilbury
Sub-sheds			Plaistow (1959-1962)
33C			1950-1962 Shoeburyness
34 Kings Cross (1950-1973)			
34A	1950-1963	KX	King's Cross
34B	1950-1961		Hornsey, became sub-shed of 34G
34C	1950-1961		Hatfield
34D	1950-1973	HI	Hitchin
34E	1950-1958		Neasden, became 14D
Sub-sheds			Aylesbury
			Chesham
	1958-1968		New England, previously 35A
Sub-shed			Spalding (to 1960)
34F	1958-1963		Grantham, previously 35B
34G	1960-1973	FP	Finsbury Park
Sub-shed			Hornsey (1961-1971)
35 Peterborough (until 1958)			
35A	1950-1958		New England, became 34E
Sub-sheds			Bourne (to 1953)
			Spalding

			Stamford (to 1957)
35B	1950-1958		Grantham, became 34F
35C	1950-1958		Peterborough Spital Bridge (was 16B 1949-1950), previously 16B, became 31F
36 Doncaster			
36A	1950-1973	DR	Doncaster
36B	1950-1958		Mexborough, became 41F
Sub-shed			Wath Electric Depot (from 1952)
36C	1950-1973	FH	Frodingham
36D	1950-1958		Barnsley, became 41G
36E	1950-1965		Retford
Sub-shed			Newark (to 1959)
37 Ardsley (until 1956)			
37A	1950-1956		Ardsley, became 56B
37B	1950-1956		Copley Hill, became 56C
37C	1950-1956		Bradford (Hammerton Street), became 56G
38 Colwick (until 1958)			
38A	1950-1958		Colwick, became 40E
Sub-shed			Derby (to 1955)
38B	1950-1958		Annesley, became 16D
38C	1950-1958		Leicester (GC), became 15E
Sub-shed			Leicester (GN)
38D	1950-1958		Staveley (GC), became 41H
38E	1950-1958		Woodford Halse, became 2G
39 Gorton (until 1958)			
39A	1950-1958		Gorton, became 9H
Sub-sheds			Hayfield
			Macclesfield
			Dinting
39B	1950-1955	DA	Darnall (Sheffield), became 41A
40 Lincoln			
40A	1950-1973	LN	Lincoln
40B	1950-1973	IM	Immingham
Sub-sheds			New Holland and Grimsby to 1960s
40C	1950-1956		Louth 40D
	1950-1958		Tuxford, became 41K
40E	1950-1958		Langwith Jn, became 41J
	1958-1966		Colwick, previously 38A, became 16B
40F	1950-1964		Boston
Sub-shed			Sleaford
41 Darnall			
41A	1950-1964	DA	Darnall (Sheffield), previously 39B, became 41B
	1964-1973	TI	Tinsley
41B	1958-1964		Sheffield Grimesthorpe, previously 19A
	1964-1965	DA	Darnall (Sheffield), previously 41B
41C	1958-1961		Sheffield (Millhouses), previously 19B
	1963-1973	WH	Wath, previously sub-shed of 41F
41D	1958-1965		Canklow, previously 19C

41E	1958-1965	BH	Staveley (Barrow Hill)
Sub-sheds			Sheepbridge
			Staveley New Works
			Staveley Old Works, previously 18D
41F	1958-1964		Mexborough, previously 36B
Sub-shed			Wath Electric Depot (1958-1963)
41G	1958-1963		Barnsley, previously 36D
41H	1958-1965		Staveley (GC), previously 38D
41J	1958-1966		Langwith Jn
40E	1966-1973	SB	Shirebrook West
41K	1958-1959		Tuxford, previously 40D
North Eastern Region			
50 York			
50A	1950-1967	YK	York, became 55B
50B	1950-1960	NL	Neville Hill
Sub-shed			Ilkley (to 1959), became 55H
	1960-1970	DC	Dairycoates (Hull) Also used for Hull (Alexandra Dock) until closed in 1963, previously 53A and 53B.
50C	1950-1959		Selby
	1960-1973	BG	Hull (Botanic Gardens)
50D	1950-1959		Starbeck
Sub-shed			Pateley Bridge (to 1951)
	1960-1973	GO	Goole
50E	1950-1963		Scarborough
50F	1950-1963		Malton
Sub-shed			Pickering (to 1959)
50G	1950-1959		Whitby
51 Darlington			
51A	1950-1973	DN	Darlington
Sub-shed			Middleton-in-Teesdale (to 1957)
51B	1950-1958		Newport
51C	1950-1967		West Hartlepool
51D	1950-1958		Middlesbrough
Sub-shed			Guisborough (to 1954)
51E	1950-1959		Stockton
51F	1950-1965		West Auckland
Sub-shed			Wearhead (to 1954)
51G	1950-1959		Haverton Hill
51H	1950-1958		Kirkby Stephen, became 12E
51J	1950-1963		Northallerton
			Leyburn (to 1954)
51K	1950-1958		Saltburn
51L	1958-1973	TE	Thornaby
52 Gateshead			
52A	1950-1973	GD	Gateshead
Sub-sheds			Bowes Bridge (to 1962)
			Heaton (1963-1967)

THE DIESEL DEPOT 29

Depot Heydays 1968-1983

BR's last roundhouse in regular use was at Barrow Hill, but it too succumbed to closure in 1982. Fortunately, it has survived and today thrives as a preservation centre and home to several rail industry companies. This is a typical line up around the turntable in 1977. (Michael Rhodes)

out of Gateshead, Thornaby and Darlington to a FIP, and the same was also considered for Healey Mills, Tinsley and Immingham, along with reducing either Cricklewood or Old Oak Common to a FIP.

In some instances, though, the changes weren't immediately noticeable. For example, when Westhouses ceased to be an FIP on March 1, 1982, locos continued to stable there and the train crew depot was unaffected.

Northwich closed in September 1982 followed by Newport Ebbw Junction in October, generating annual savings in staff and overheads of £25,000 and £90,000 respectively.

			North Blyth (1967)
52B	1950-1963	HT	Heaton, became sub-shed of 52A
52C	1950-1965		Blaydon
Sub-sheds			Alston (to 1959)
			Hexham (to 1959)
			Reedsmouth (to 1952)
52D	1950-1969		Tweedmouth
Sub-shed			Alnmouth (to 1966)
52E	1950-1966		Percy Main
52F	1950-1967		North Blyth
Sub-sheds			Rothbury (to 1952)
			South Blyth (1967), became sub-shed of 52A
52G	1958-1967	SK	Sunderland
Sub-shed			Durham (1958), previously 54A
52H	1958-1967		Tyne Dock, previously 54B
52J	1958-1959		Borough Gardens, previously 54C
	1964-1973	GF	South Gosforth
52K	1958-1965		Consett

53 Hull (until 1960)

53A	1950-1960		Hull (Dairycoates), became 50B
53B	1950-1960		Hull (Botanic Gardens), became 50C
53C	1950-1960		Hull (Alexandra Dock) Included Springhead until 1958
53D	1950-1958		Bridlington
53E	1950-1951		Cudworth
	1956-1960	GO	Goole, previously 25C, became 50D

54 Sunderland (until 1958)

54A	1950-1958	SK	Sunderland
Sub-shed			Durham, became 52G
54B	1950-1958		Tyne Dock
Sub-shed			Pelton Level, became 52H
54C	1950-1958		Borough Gardens, became 52J
54D	1950-1958		Consett, became 52K

55 Leeds Holbeck (from 1957)

55A	1957-1973	HO	Leeds (Holbeck)
Sub-shed			Stourton (1967-c1972), previously 20A
55B	1957-1967		Stourton, became sub-shed of 55A
	1957-1973	YK	York, previously 50A
55C	1956-1966		Farnley Jn, previously 25G
	1967-1973	HM	Healey Mills, previously 56B
55D	1957-1971		Royston, previously 20C
55E	1957-1967		Normanton, previously 20D
55F	1957-1967		Manningham (Bradford), previously 20E
	1967-1973	HS	Hammerton Street (Bradford), previously 56G
55G	1957-1967		Huddersfield, previously 25B
	1967-1973	KY	Knottingley, previously 56A

56 Wakefield/Knottingley (from 1956)

56A	1956-1967		Wakefield, previously 25A
	1967-1973	KY	Knottingley, became KY 56B
	1956-1965		Ardsley, previously 37A
	1966-1967	HM	Healey Mills, became 55C
56C	1956-1964		Copley Hill, previously 37B
56D	1956-1967		Mirfield, previously 25D
56E	1956-1964		Sowerby Bridge, previously 25E
56F	1956-1967		Low Moor, previously 25F, became 55J
56G	1956-1958	HS	Hammerton Street (Bradford), previously 37C, became 55F

Scottish Region

60 Inverness

60A	1950-1973	IS	Inverness
Sub-sheds			Dingwall (to 1962)
			Fortrose (to 1951)
			Kyle of Lochalsh (to 1962)
60B	1950-1966		Aviemore
Sub-shed			Boat of Garten Now used by the Strathspey Railway
60C	1950-1964		Helmsdale
Sub-sheds			Dornoch (to 1960)
			Tain (to 1959)
60D	1950-1962		Wick
Sub-shed			Thurso
60E	1950-1964		Forres

61 Aberdeen

61A	1950-1967	AB	Kittybrewster (Aberdeen)
Sub-sheds			Alford
			Ballater (to 1966)
			Fraserburgh (to 1965)
			Macduff (to 1951)
			Peterhead (to 1965)
61B	1950-1966	AB	Aberdeen (Ferryhill)
61C	1950-1966		Keith
Sub-sheds			Banff (to 1964)
			Elgin

62 Thornton Jn

62A	1950-1969		Thornton Jn
Sub-sheds			Anstruther (to 1960)
			Burntisland
			Ladybank
			Methil
62B	1950-1967		Dundee Tay Bridge
Sub-sheds			Arbroath (to 1959)
			Dundee West (to 1963)
			Montrose
			St. Andrews (to 1960)
			Tayport (to 1951)

	1967-1973	DE	Dundee, former Dundee West reopened
62C	1950-1966	DT	Dunfermline
Sub-sheds		DT	Alloa (to 1967)
			Inverkeithing
			Kelty (to c.1955)
			Loch Leven (to 1951)

63 Perth

63A	1950-1969	PH	Perth
Sub-sheds			Aberfeldy (to 1965)
			Blair Atholl (to 1965)
			Crieff (to 1958)
			Forfar (1959-1964)
63B	1950-1960		Stirling, became 65J
Sub-sheds			Killin
			Stirling Shore Road
	1960-1970		Fort William, previously 65J, became 65H
Sub-shed			Mallaig (to 1961)
63C	1950-1959		Forfar, became sub-shed of 63A
Sub-shed			Brechin
			Ballaculish
	1959-1963		Oban, previously 63D
Sub-shed			Ballachulish
63D	1950-1955		Fort William, became 65J
	1955-1959		Oban, previously 63E, became 63C
Sub-shed			Ballachulish
63E	1950-1955		Oban, became 63D
Sub-shed			Ballachulish

64 St Margarets/Millerhill

64A	1950-1967		St Margarets (Edinburgh)
Sub-sheds			Dunbar (to 1963)
			Galashiels (to c.1962)
			Hardengreen
			Leith Central (1955 to 1959)
			Longniddry
			North Berwick (to 1958)
			Peebles (to 1955)
			Penicuik (to 1951)
			Polton (to 1955)
			Seafield (to 1962)
			South Leith (to 1955)
	1967-1973	MH	Millerhill
64B	1950-1973	HA	Haymarket
64C	1950-1965		Dalry Road
64D	1950-1960		Carstairs, became 66E
64E	1950-1960		Polmont
Sub-shed			Kinneil, became 65K
64F	1950-1966		Bathgate
64G	1950-1966		Hawick

Depot Heydays 1968-1983

Stabling points

While the steam era did have a small amount of what today would be called servicing points, to provide coal and water, the diesel era saw the proliferation of the stabling point and small servicing sheds. Weekday stabling points included King's Cross, so locos could receive basic attention before embarking upon their next service. It was the weekend when most stabling points came into their own and places such as Aberdare, Coalville, Perth and Worksop would see dozens of locos congregate without depot facilities.

Remote depots, such as Holyhead, were considered 'safe' for many years, but the arrival of modern DMUs and the loss of freight work eventually saw them become redundant. Class 40 40129 stands outside the depot building on February 22, 1975. (Chris Booth)

Changing times

It may be seen that while the aftermath of the miners' strike is often cited as resulting in several BR depot closures, in reality BR had already begun a rationalisation programme. Despite a drop from 169 collieries to fewer than 86 by 1986, the UK was still producing around 100m tonnes of coal per annum and, in the 1980s at least, colliery closures resulted in few direct depot closures. What was more damaging at the time to the diesel depots were the closure programmes already outlined, along with significant changes to working practices that were being pushed through. In 1982, ASLEF and BR fought a war by proxy on behalf of the Conservative Government and the trade union. Pushed by the government to achieve cost savings and efficiency gains, BR sought to eradicate the 1919 agreement of an eight-hour day for drivers. It also sought to introduce a more flexible rostering agreement that would allow shift start times to be brought forward or delayed by up to several hours. Such changes were designed to make drivers more efficient and actually drive for longer proportions of the shift duration, consequently reducing BR's driver requirement and thus ultimately the number of depots it would need.

The second significant change at this time was the move towards Driver Only Operation, or DOO as it became known. Throughout the 1970s most freight trains required a secondman and guard, and so even

Sub-sheds			Jedburgh (1950)
			Kelso (to 1955)
			Riccarton (to 1958)
			St Boswells (to 1959)
64H	1959-1972		Leith Central, previously sub-shed of 64A
65 Eastfield			
65A	1950-1973	ED	Eastfield (Glasgow)
Sub-sheds			Aberfoyle (to 1951)
			Helensburgh (1960-1961)
			Kilsyth (to 1951)
			Kipps (1962)
			Lennoxtown (to 1951)
			Motherwell (from 1972)
			Parkhead (1962)
			Polmadie (from 1972)
65B	1950-1966		St Rollox
65C	1950-1962		Parkhead, became sub-shed of 65A
65D	1950-1964		Dawsholm
Sub-sheds			Dumbarton
			Stobcross (1950)
65E	1950-1962		Kipps, became sub-shed of 65A
65F	1950-1973	GM	Grangemouth
65G	1950-1964		Yoker
65H	1950-1960		Helensburgh, became sub-shed of 65A
Sub-shed			Arrochar (to c.1959)
	1970-1973	FW	Fort William, previously 63B
65I	1950-1961		Balloch
65J	1950-1960		Fort William
Sub-shed			Mallaig, previously 63D, became 63B
65K	1960-1964		Polmont, previously 64E
66 Polmadie			
66A	1950-1972	PO	Polmadie, became sub-shed of 65A
Sub-sheds			Motherwell (from 1967)
			Paisley
66B	1950-1963		Motherwell
Sub-shed			Morningside (to 1954), became sub-shed of 66A
66C	1950-1973	HN	Hamilton
66D	1950-1966		Greenock (Ladyburn)
Sub-shed			Princes Pier (to 1959)
66E	1960-1963		Carstairs, previously 64D, reopened 1966-1967 then, became a stabling point 66F 1962-1967 BP Beattock, previously 68D
67 Corkerhill			
67A	1950-1973	CK	Corkerhill
67B	1950-1966		Hurlford
Sub-sheds			Beith
			Muirkirk (to 1964)
67C	1950-1973	AY	Ayr

67D	1950-1973		Ardrossan
67E	1962-1966		Dumfries, previously 68B
67F	1962-1968		Stranraer, previously 68C
68 Carlisle Kingmoor			
68A	1950-1966	KD	Carlisle (Kingmoor)
Sub-shed			Durran Hill, became 12A
68B	1950-1962		Dumfries
Sub-shed			Kirkcudbright (to 1955), became 67E
68C	1950-1962		Stranraer
Sub-shed			Newton Stewart (to 1959), became 67F
68D	1950-1962		Beattock
Sub-shed			Lockerbie (to 1951), became 66F
68E	1951-1958		Carlisle Canal, previously 12B, became 12D

Southern Region

70 Nine Elms			
70A	1950-1967		Nine Elms
70B	1950-1970		Feltham
70C	1950-1967		Guildford
Sub-shed			Reading S.R. (1962-1964)
70D	1950-1963		Basingstoke
	1963-1973	EH	Eastleigh, previously 71A
Sub-sheds			Fratton
			Lymington (to 1967)
			Southampton Docks (from 1966)
70E	1950-1962	RG	Reading (SR), became sub-shed of 70C
	1962-1967		Salisbury, previously 72B
70F	1954-1959	FR	Fratton, became sub-shed of 71A
	1963-1973	BM	Bournemouth, previously 71B
70G	1954-1957		Newport (IOW), previously 71E
	1963-1967		Weymouth, previously 82F
70H	1954-1973		Ryde (IOW), became RY
70I	1950-1966		Southampton Docks, previously 71I, became sub-shed of 70D
71 Eastleigh (until 30 September 1963)			
71A	1950-1966	ED	Eastleigh, became 70D
Sub-sheds			Andover Jn (to 1957)
			Fratton (from 1959)
			Lymington (to 1967)
			Southampton Terminus (to 1967)
			Winchester (to 1969)
71B	1950-1963	BM	Bournemouth, became 70F
Sub-sheds			Dorchester (1955-1957)
			Hamworthy Jn (to 1954)
			Swanage (to 1966)
71C	1950-1955		Dorchester, became sub-shed of 71B
71D	1950-1954		Fratton
Sub-sheds			Gosport (to 1953), became 70F

71E	1950-1954		Newport (IOW), became 70G
71F	1950-1954		Ryde (IOW), became 70H
71G	1950-1958		Bath (S&D)
Sub-sheds			Branksome
			Radstock, became 82F
	1958-1963		Weymouth, previously 82F, became 70G
71H	1950-1958		Templecombe (S&D)
Sub-sheds			Highbridge (to c.1955), became 82G
	1958-1959		Yeovil Pen Mill, previously 82E
71I	1950-1963		Southampton Docks, became 70I
71J	c1955-1958		Highbridge, became sub-shed of 82F
72 Exmouth Jn			
72A	1950-1966		Exmouth Jn, became 83D
Sub-sheds			Bude
			Exmouth
			Launceston (to c.1958)
			Lyme Regis
			Okehampton (to c.1961)
			Seaton (to 1963)
72B	1950-1962		Salisbury, became 70E
72C	1950-1963		Yeovil, became 83E
72D	1950-1958		Plymouth Friary
Sub-shed			Callington, became 83H
72E	1950-1963		Barnstaple
Sub-sheds			Ilfracombe
			Torrington (to 1959), became 83F
72F	1950-1963		Wadebridge, became 84E
73 Stewarts Lane/Hither Green			
73A	1950-1962	SL	Stewarts Lane, became 75D
73B	1950-1962		Bricklayers' Arms
Sub-sheds			New Cross Gate (to 1952)
73C	1950-1973	HG	Hither Green
Sub-shed			Redhill (1965-?)
73D	1950-1959	GI	Gillingham, became sub-shed of 73J
	1963-1973	SE	St Leonards, became SE
73E	1950-1964		Faversham
73F	1950-1973	AF	Ashford
Sub-sheds			Ramsgate (locomotives, 1959-1960)
			St Leonards (to 1963)
			Tonbridge (1962-1965)
73G	1950-1973	RM	Ramsgate, previously 74B; EMUs only from 1959
73H	1958-1961		Dover, previously 74C
Sub-sheds			Folkestone (to 1961)
73J	1958-1965		Tonbridge, became sub-shed of 73F
Sub-shed			Gillingham(1959-1960)
74 Ashford (until 13 October 1958)			
74A	1950-1958		Ashford, became 73F
Sub-sheds			Canterbury West (to 1955)

THE DIESEL DEPOT | 31

Depot Heydays 1968-1983

Glasgow's Polmadie Depot was home to around 90 locos in the early 1970s, but as traffic reduced it lost its importance, with many duties taken over by Eastfield and Motherwell. In this view taken in March 1974 are (l-r) an unidentified Class 47, Class 27 5365, Class 24 5096, Class 20 8179, Class 45 19, Class 40 40186, and two Class 50s (426 at the front). (Rail Photoprints)

a depot with only a dozen turns still needed around 40 men. Coal traffic especially had radically changed between the late 1960s and early 1980s. The yards and collieries were no longer full of rakes of unfitted and vacuum-braked 16 ton mineral wagons and 21 ton hoppers. Thanks mainly to the Class 20s and 47s, followed by Type 5 power in the form of Class 56 and the imminently introduced Class 58, the MGR principle not only drastically slashed wagon numbers, it also made the drivers and train crews far more efficient in transporting larger tonnages of coal in less time. Guards were dispensed with on the air-braked MGRs, and on the ground the shunters' jobs all but ceased except for run rounds, which allowed the trainman grade to replace guards and shunters. It was these efficiency gains that drastically reduced the number of staff needed at each depot, thus bringing about the closure of facilities such as Wath in January 1983 when its work was taken over by Healey Mills, Tinsley, Doncaster and Knottingley men.

			Rolvenden (to 1954)
			St Leonards (1958)
74B	1950-1958		Ramsgate, became 73G
74C	1950-1958	DV	Dover
Sub-sheds			Folkestone, became 73H
74D	1950-1958		Tonbridge, became 73J
74E	1950-1958		St Leonards, became sub-shed of 74A
75 Brighton			
75A	1950-1973	BI	Brighton
Sub-sheds			Eastbourne (1952-1965)
			Horsham (1959-1964)
			Newhaven (to 1955)
			Three Bridges (1964-1965)
			Tunbridge Wells West (1963-1965)
75B	1950-1965		Redhill, became sub-shed of 73C
Sub-sheds			Tunbridge Wells West (1965)
75C	1950-1966		Norwood Jn
	1966-1973	SU	Selhurst
75D	1950-1959		Horsham, became sub-shed of 75A
	1962-1973	SL	Stewarts Lane, previously 73A
75E	1950-1964		Three Bridges, became sub-shed of 75A
75F	1950-1963	TW	Tunbridge Wells West, became sub-shed of 75A, later 75B
75G	1950-1952		Eastbourne, became sub-shed of 75A

Western Region

81 London			
81A	1950-1973	OC	Old Oak Common
Sub-shed			Southall (1968-1973)
81B	1950-1964		Slough
Sub-sheds			Aylesbury (1950)
			Marlow (to 1962)
			Watlington (to 1957)
81C	1950-1968		Southall
Sub-shed			Staines (to 1952)
81D	1950-1973	RG	Reading
Sub-sheds			Basingstoke WR (1950)
			Henley-on-Thames (to 1958)
81E	1950-1965		Didcot
Sub-sheds			Newbury
			Wallingford (to 1956)
			Winchester Chesil (to 1953)
81F	1950-1973	OX	Oxford
Sub-sheds			Abingdon (to 1954)
			Fairford (to 1962)
82 Bristol			
82A	1950-1973	BR	Bristol, Bath Road
Sub-sheds			Bath (to 1961)
			Taunton (from 1968)

			Wells (to 1963)
			Westbury (from 1968)
			Weston-super-Mare (to 1960)
			Yatton (to 1960)
82B	1950-1964	PM	St Philips Marsh
82C	1950-1973	SW	Swindon
Sub-sheds			Andover Jn (to 1952)
			Chippenham (to 1964)
			Malmesbury (to 1951)
			Marlborough (to 1961)
			Faringdon (to 1951)
82D	1950-1963		Westbury, became 83C
Sub-sheds			Frome
			Salisbury WR (1950)
82E	1950-1958		Yeovil Pen Mill, became 71H
	1958-1965		Bristol, Barrow Road, previously 22A
82F	1950-1958		Weymouth, became 71G
Sub-shed			Bridport
	1958-1966		Bath S&D
Sub-sheds			Branksome (to 1963)
			Highbridge (1958)
			Radstock, previously 71G
82G	1958-1963		Templecombe, previously 71H, became 83G
83 Newton Abbot			
83A	1950-1973	NA	Newton Abbot
Sub-sheds			Ashburton (to 1958)
			Kingsbridge (to 1961)
			Tiverton Jn (1963-1964)
83B	1950-1968		Taunton
Sub-sheds			Barnstaple Town (to 1951)
			Bridgwater (to 1960)
			Minehead (to 1956)
83C	1950-1963	EX	Exeter
Sub-sheds			Tiverton Jn
	1963-1968		Westbury
83D	1950-1963		Plymouth, Laira, became 84A
Sub-sheds			Launceston (1958-1962)
			Plymouth Docks (to c1951)
			Princetown (to 1956)
	1963-1967		Exmouth Jn, previously 72A
Sub-sheds			Bude (to 1964)
			Callington (1963)
			Exmouth (1963)
			Lyme Regis (1963)
			Seaton (1963)
83E	1950-1963	BZ	St Blazey, became 84B
Sub-sheds			(to 1962), Looe
			Moorswater (to 1960)
	1963-1965		Yeovil Town, previously 72C
83F	1950-1963		Truro, became 84C

	1963-1964		Barnstaple Jn
Sub-shed			Ilfracombe, previously 72E
83G	1950-1963	PZ	Penzance, became 84D
Sub-sheds			Helston
			St Ives (to 1961)
	1963-1966		Templecombe, previously 82G
83H	1958-1963		Plymouth Friary, previously 72D
Sub-shed			Callington
84 Wolverhampton (until 1963) Plymouth (from 1963)			
84A	1950-1963		Wolverhampton, Stafford Road
	1963-1973	LA	Plymouth, Laira, previously 83D, became LA
84B	1950-1963		Wolverhampton, Oxley, became 2B
	1963-1973	BZ	St Blazey, previously 83E
84C	1950-1963		Banbury, became 2D
	1963-1965		Truro, previously 83F
84D	1950-1963		Leamington Spa, became 2L
	1963-1973	PZ	Penzance, previously 83G
Sub-shed			Helston (1963)
84E	1950-1963		Tyseley, became 2A
84F	1950-1963		Stourbridge Jn, became 2C
84G	1950-1961		Shrewsbury, became 89A
Sub-sheds			Builth Road
			Clee Hill (to 1960)
			Coalport
			Craven Arms
			Knighton
			Ludlow (to 1951)
	1961-1963		Kidderminster, previously 85D, became 2P
Sub-shed			Cleobury Mortimer (to 1962)
84H	1950-1963		Wellington (Salop)
Sub-sheds		CG	Crewe Gresty Lane, became 2M
			Much Wenlock (to 1951)
84J	1950-1961		Croes Newydd, became 89B
Sub-sheds			Bala
			Penmaenpool
			Trawsfynydd
84K	1950-1958	CH	Chester, became 6E
	1958-1960		Wrexham Rhosddu, previously 6E
85 Worcester			
85A	1950-1973	WS	Worcester
Sub-sheds			Evesham (to 1963)
			Hartlebury
			Honeybourne (to 1965)
			Kingham (to 1962)
			Ledbury (1961-1964)
			Moreton in Marsh
85B	1950-1973	GL	Gloucester, Horton Road
Sub-sheds			Brimscombe (to 1963)
			Chalford (to 1951)

Depot Heydays 1968-1983

Plymouth Laira was an early home to the Western Region's diesel hydraulic fleet and then an increasing number of Class 50s. It remains an important depot for Great Western Railway, servicing and maintaining much of the firm's HST fleet. Five Class 50s and three Class 47s are visible in this shot taken on April 25, 1982. (Colour-Rail)

Conclusion

Between the eradication of steam and 1980, BR's total number of traction depots and servicing points/loco inspection points stayed roughly the same. The railway was changing and modernising, however, and with the introduction of Type 5 freight power the MGR revolution massively streamlined the movement of coal. This, along with diminishing freight tonnages and the HST, made inroads into BR's passenger loco requirement, notably the Deltics and eventually the Peaks and Class 47s. Thus with sectorisation looming, between January 1981 and December 1984 BR's loco fleet was reduced by 16.6%, and while the depot closures and status reductions sounded like drastic proposals, depot rationalisation merely reflected the changing times; maintenance facilities were reduced by a slightly larger 17.3%. A national rationalisation and closure programme was about to begin, but BR sent internal memos asking its managers to be careful about the proposals and moves towards closing depots so that the unions didn't realise that a national review was already underway. DD

			Cheltenham Malvern Road (to 1963)
			Cirencester (to 1964)
			Lydney (to 1964)
			Tetbury (to 1964)
85C Sub-sheds	1950-1961		Hereford, became 86C
			Kington (to 1951)
			Ledbury
			Leominster
			Ross-on-Wye
	1961-1964		Gloucester Barnwood, previously 85E
			Dursley (to 1962)
			Tewkesbury (to 1962)
85D Sub-shed	1950-1961		Kidderminster
			Cleobury Mortimer, became 84G
	1961-1964		Bromsgrove
Sub-shed			Redditch, previously 85F
85E Sub-sheds	1958-1961		Gloucester, Barnwood, became 85C
			Dursley
			Tewkesbury, previously 22B
85F Sub-shed	1958-1961		Bromsgrove, became 85D
			Redditch, previously 21C
86 Newport/Cardiff			
86A	1950-1963	EJ	Newport, Ebbw Jn, became 86B
	1963-1973	CF	Cardiff Canton, previously 86C
86B	1950-1963		Newport, Pill
	1963-1973	EJ	Newport, Ebbw Jn, previously 86A
86C	1950-1961	CF	Cardiff, Canton, became 88A
	1961-1964	HF	Hereford, previously 85C
86D	1950-1961		Llantrisant, became 88G
86E	1950-1968	ST	Severn Tunnel Jn
86F	1950-1961		Tondu, became 88H
Sub-shed			Bridgend (1950)
	1961-1964		Aberbeeg, previously 86H
86G	1950-1967		Pontypool Road
Sub-sheds			Abergavenny (1954-1958)
			Branches Fork (to 1952)
			Pontrilas (to 1953)
86H	1950-1961		Aberbeeg, became 86F
86J	1950-1961		Aberdare, became 88J
86K	1950-1954		Abergavenny
Sub-shed			Tredegar
	1954-1960		Tredegar
87 Neath/Swansea			
87A Sub-sheds	1950-1965		Neath, Court Sart
			Glyn Neath (to 1964)
			Neath
			Bridge Street (to 1964)
	1969-1973	LE	Swansea, Landore, previously 87E
87B	1950-1964		Port Talbot, Duffryn Yard

	1964-1973	MG	Margam
87C	1950-1964		Swansea, Danygraig
87D	1950-1964		Swansea, East Dock
Sub-sheds			Gurnos (1959-1962)
			Upper Bank (1959-1962)
87E	1950-1969		Swansea, Landore, became 87A
87F	1950-1965		Llanelli
Sub-sheds			Burry Port (to 1962)
			Llandovery (1959-1964)
			Pantyffynon (to 1964)
87G	1950-1964		Carmarthen
Sub-shed			Newcastle Emlyn (to 1952)
87H	1950-1963		Neyland
Sub-sheds			Cardigan (to 1962)
			Milford Haven (to 1962)
			Pembroke Dock
			Whitland 1963-1969
			Whitland
87J	1950-1963		Fishguard
87K	1950-1959		Swansea, Victoria
Sub-sheds			Gurnos
			Llandovery
			Upper Bank (1950-1957)
88 Cardiff			
88A	1950-1957		Cardiff (Cathays)
Sub-shed			Radyr
	1957-1961		Radyr, became 88B
Sub-shed			Cardiff Cathays
	1961-1963	CF	Cardiff Canton, previously 86C, became 86A
Sub-shed			Cardiff East Dock (1961-1962)
88B	1950-1961		Cardiff East Dock, became 88L
	1961-1962		Cardiff Cathays, previously 88A, became 88M
Sub-shed			Radyr
	1962-1968		Radyr
88C	1950-1964	BA	Barry
88D	1950-1964		Merthyr Tydfil
Sub-sheds			Dowlais Cae Harris
			Dowlais Central (to 1960)
			Rhymney
	1964-1965		Rhymney
88E	1950-1964		Abercynon
88F	1950-1967		Treherbert
Sub-sheds			Ferndale (to 1964)
			Pwllyrhebog (to 1951)
88G	1961-1964		Llantrisant, previously 86B
88H	1961-1964		Tondu, previously 86F
88J	1961-1965		Aberdare, previously 86F
88K	1961-1962		Brecon, previously 89B; no loco allocation after 1959

88L	1962-1963		Cardiff East Dock, previously 88B and sub-shed of 88A
88M	1962-1964		Cardiff Cathays, previously 88B
89 Oswestry (until 1963)			
89A Sub-sheds	1950-1961		Oswestry
			Llanfylin (to 1952)
			Landiloes (to 1962), became 89D
	1961-1963		Shrewsbury, previously 84G, became 6D
89B Sub-shed	1950-1959		Brecon
			Builth Wells (to 1957)
	1961-1963		Croes Newydd, previously 84J, became 6C
89C Sub-sheds	1950-1963		Machynlleth, became 6F
			Aberayron (to 1962)
			Aberystwyth
			Aberystwyth VoR
			Portmadoc
			Pwllheli
89D	1961-1963		Oswestry, previously 89A, became 6E

AF	Ashford Chart Leacon		CT	Cleethorpes
BA	Crewe Basford Hall		CT	Chester WRD
BB	Beachbrook Farm EWS		CU	Carlisle Currock WRD
BC	Beachbrook Farm Freightliner		CV	Cardiff Canton DMU
BC	MoD Bicester		CX	Crofton (Bombardier)
BD	Birkenhead North (12/76)		CZ	Central Rivers
BG	Billingham		CY	Clapham Jn
BH	Barrow Hill Museum		DF	Derby FM Rail
BH	Billingham ICI		DI	Didcot (GW Society)
BJ	Bristol Marsh Jn		DL	Doncaster Major Level 5, to ZF
BK	Birkenhead Central		DL	Dollands Moor
BK	Bristol Barton Hill (from 06/92)		DM	Dagenham Dock
BL	Blyth Cambois		DM	Dee Marsh
BL	Basford Hall (Freightliner)		DT	Didcot
BN	Birkenhead North		EA	East Anglia Railway Museum
BN	Bounds Green (from 12/76)		EC	Edinburgh Craigentinny
BQ	Bury/Heywood		EL	East Lancashire Railway, Heywood
BT	Bo'ness Scottish RPS			
CB	Codnor Park (Midland Railway Trust)		EM	East Ham
CB	Crewe Basford Hall		EN	Euston Downside Carriage Sidings
CB	Crewebrook Sidings		EP	Derby Etches Park, became DY
CC	Crewe Carriage Sidings		EP	Edinburgh Portobello (Wheel Lathe), EU Eurre (France Class 37s paper allocation)
CE	Crewe Electric			
CG	Croxley Green		ET	Eastleigh Freightliner
CJ	Clapham Jn Carriage Sidings		EU	Euston Station
CL	Glasgow Cowlairs		EU	East Usk
CO	Coquelles (France)		FB	Ferrybridge
CO	Cranmore (East Somerset Railway)		FD	Freightliner Diesel paper allocation
CP	Crewe CS (LNWR Co Ltd)			
CQ	Crewe (The Railway Age)		FE	Freightliner Electric paper allocation
CS	Carnforth (WCRC)			

THE DIESEL DEPOT 33

Old Oak Common

The steam shed

The late 19th century growth of the Great Western main line meant that the Great Western Railway (GWR) was in need of a larger facility than the 1855-built Westbourne Park shed that had previously supplied many of the GWR's locomotives and carriages. A site in South Acton was purchased in 1901 and work began on a shed designed by George Jackson Churchward. It came into full use from March 17, 1906 and was the head of the GWR London operating division as well as being the largest depot on the GWR system. It also set the pattern for other depots throughout the company's territory, including Tyseley. The loco sheds measured 444ft by 360ft and had four electrically powered 65ft

Old Oak Common

turntables. Each one had 28 radiating lines with a pit, able to accommodate locos up to 75ft and thus 112 locos could be housed under cover. On the eastern side of the depot there was a lifting and repair shop termed 'The Factory'. Its Welsh slate roof was supported by wood and steel rafters, and it had London Brick Company walls. A traverser gave access to the building's 12 roads. As well as the usual carpenters, blacksmiths, offices and general stores, it also had a 50 ton crane.

Early diesels

The first allocated diesel was a GWR shunter in October 1936, which was visually similar to a Class 08, and it stayed until September 1939. It returned in November 1947 and was renumbered 15100 in March 1948. Before World War Two a diesel refuelling stage for GWR railcars was added just north of the repair shop. At nationalisation on January 1, 1948 the depot had an allocation of 231 locos. The GWR ordered a further six diesel shunters and these arrived between March and July the same year. They became BR Class D3/11s, and were all allocated to Old Oak until late 1958.

On February 1, 1950 the shed was designated 81A and gas turbine loco 18000 arrived in May that year, followed by 18100 two years later; they left in December 1960 and January 1958 respectively. Southern Railway shunter 15202 had a two-year stay at the shed between April 1951 and October 1953 when the first of the BR 350hp 0-6-0 shunters (13030-3) arrived. By 1959 the depot had seven diesels and an allocation of 160 steam engines.

Main line diesels

A large number of 0-6-0 shunters came and went from Old Oak, with 1960 alone seeing 24 different examples transfer in and out. Ultimately, 75 different shunters had been allocated to the depot by December 1974. In September 1962 the first allocated diesel hydraulic Westerns (later Class 52s), D1007/8/9 arrived and by December D1000-13 and D1036-45 were all based there. By January 1964 all of the class, except for D1050/2/4/5/6/7/8/9/64/66/7/9/70, had been on the depot's books.

The first Brush Type 4s (later Class 47) arrived in October 1963 and they would go on to become by far the most numerous main line class, with 92 different examples being allocated by December 1974. In May 1963, the first Hymeks (later Class 35), D7076 and D7078, came, and a further 57 classmates had followed by October 1974. Four of what became Class 14 (D9521-4) were based there between November 1964 and October 1965, and 26 North British Type 2s (later Class 22 and often called 'Baby Warships') were allocated between September 1963 and June 1969, although D6356 made a brief return from February 1970 until May 1971.

The first resident Class 43 Warships came in July 1967 and by the time the last had left in October 1970, 25 had received an allocation at some point. D5528 was the first Brush Type 2 (later Class 31) to be based at the West London depot, arriving in March 1969, and although it left in March 1973, 28 examples had been based there by December 1974.

Full dieselisation

With plans for the rundown of steam on the GWR nearing completion, the reconstruction of Old Oak Common as a diesel depot began in 1964. It was the last of the Western Region's six large diesel depots, the others being Plymouth Laira, Bristol Bath Road and Margam in 1960, Landore in 1962 and finally Cardiff Canton in 1964. The majority of the GWR 1906 depot had been demolished by early 1965 and the final dozen or so steam locos were transferred away to Southall when the shed closed to steam on March 22, 1965. When the steam sheds were knocked down one of the turntables was retained and the stabling of diesels around it became

LEFT: Two Met-Cammell Pullman power cars (60091 and 60099) stand proud of the Pullman shed at Old Oak Common on July 24, 1974. (David Hird)

THE DIESEL DEPOT | 35

Old Oak Common

LEFT: GWR 0-6-0PT tank 9706 inside one of Old Oak's roundhouses before steam was ousted on the Western Region. With the arrival of the diesels all four roundhouses and three of the turntables were removed. (Brian Morrison)

BELOW LEFT: A classic view of the Old Oak Common turntable in the late 1970s. By this time several of the turntable roads had been taken out of use, although it could still hold a useful number of locos.
(Michael Rhodes)

quite a feature. The Factory repair shop and parts of the stores were also kept.

Changes for diesels in the Factory saw it become the base for heavy repairs and some of the inspection pits were lengthened and deepened, with jacks provided to allow for bogie and spring changing. A notable feature of the Factory's heavy lifting jacks was that they were wheeled into position along their own rails inset into the concrete floor. Outside the Factory the traverser was removed and the number of roads reduced to seven, which were all directly accessible. A new three-road servicing shed was built and it undertook all servicing and A-exams as well as fuelling and watering. Each line held two locos, fuel supply points, inspection pits and a washing plant on the approach road. Outside the Factory stood a cleaning shed that was affectionately known as the 'elephant house' and it had pressure jets for cleaning loco roofs, sides and underframes simultaneously.

When the Blue Pullman fixed-formation DMUs were introduced in the 1960s, the 1935-built carriage maintenance building was converted for their use. After the Pullmans were withdrawn in the 1970s the shed became the depot's paint shop. In the late 1980s the paint shop housed a 75 ton telescopic jib diesel hydraulic crane ADRC96712, along with mess and dormitory coach ADB975574, tool and generator van ADB975613 and tool van ADB975613.

On May 6, 1973 the depot was coded OC under TOPS, and later in the 1970s the new HST Depot became OO, while the coach depot became OM.

Open days

The depot held more open days than perhaps any other in the country. Its first took place on July 15, 1967 and others in September 1972, August 1980, September 1981 and 1985, March 1987, August 1991 and finally March 1994. The 1985 event was notable for seeing the return of old favourites – green liveried Hymek D7018 and Class 52 D1015 *Western Champion* in golden ochre livery, both being displayed in the Factory alongside green liveried 47500 *Great Western* and 50007 *Sir Edward Elgar* to mark the 150th anniversary of the GWR.

Shunters

In August 1979, Old Oak's Class 08s had diagrams for air-braked examples at Park Royal Freight Depot, the HST depot pilot, two or three at Acton Yard and three in the carriage sidings (A, C and D Pilots), one of which also covered Paddington's parcels sidings in the evening and throughout the night (A Pilot). Further afield, 08s were based at West Drayton and Southall Yard, along with one at Slough Yard. Occasional duties also covered West Ealing CCE Yard and trips of fuel tanks to Ranelagh Bridge stabling point. By May 1987 the dozen shunter diagrams had been halved to just six, although three still worked in and around the depot as pilot engines at the TMD, HST Depot and carriage sidings.

In July 1989, the FSSO Pool of Railfreight Distribution was established and contained eight different 08s until it

ABOVE LEFT: Class 31 31230 and 47509 receive attention in the Factory during the late 1970s. Three shifts of two footplate crewmen were assigned to the 'Pullman' duty that moved locos in and out of the factory. (Michael Rhodes)

LEFT: Western Region Gas Turbine 18000 stands outside the Factory at Old Oak Common on May 12, 1957. (Rail Photoprints/Dave Cobbe Collection – C R L Coles)

Old Oak Common

ABOVE: Class 47 1669 *Python* (nameplate removed) outside the servicing shed in 1974. It appears to have just received a new set of brake blocks, one of the frequent jobs undertaken while locos were fuelled and watered. (Chris Booth)

BELOW: The Old Oak Common Factory had the ability to lift locos for repairs and bogie changes/examinations. Illustrated is 50025 *Invincible*, jacked so its bogies could be removed on November 26, 1985. Rail Photoprints/Brian Robbins

Personal observations

During my five years at Old Oak Common I worked with some fascinating characters. Many were 'old school' former steam drivers with a wealth of experience, which most were happy to pass on to the young Driver's Assistants, as our former Secondman position had been renamed. I particularly remember Alfie Franklin, or 'Woodbine' as he was affectionately known, who quickly worked out who he could trust to 'have a go' and put me in the hot seat on many an occasion, even all the way from Exeter to Paddington once. Other real characters included 'Fast Eddie' and 'Fangs Dyer', the latter more memorable for his questionable personal hygiene unfortunately.

One of the more interesting turns that usually stayed within the confines of the depot was the 'Pullman'. There were three shifts (0700-1500, 1500-2300 and 2300-0700) of a Driver and Driver's Assistant and their job was to move locos to and from the Factory for repairs, often requiring dead locos to be shunted about. It certainly helped you to practice your coupling skills and a week on any shift was guaranteed to beef up the arm muscles! Pullman crews were often called upon to take a loco light engine off the depot to rescue a failure out on the main line. I can remember one week on the 1500 turn when we were tasked to go and rescue failed Class 50s three days in a row, one on the down main right in front of Old Oak Panel box, one on the down main at West Ealing and the last one on the up main at Hayes & Harlington. This was prior to the Class 50 refurbishment programme, when they were not the most reliable of locos.

Most crews will probably agree that the 'workabus' trips between the depot and Paddington could be the most stressful part of the whole shift, if your turn required the use of one. Most of the minibus drivers were West Indian and included some real characters with appropriate nicknames – 'Sidesaddle' should give you hint at how one drove! The old Ford Transits were often thrashed to death, particularly by 'Fordy'; depending on his mood on the day you often took your life in your hands, and I know of several men who wouldn't ride with him.

Fond memories though, but I lamented the recent demolition of the site as so little remains of the WR's former diesel depots.

Mark Nicholls
Editor

A Class 08 drags 47484 *Isambard Kingdom Brunel* from the Factory. The wiring emerging from the cab window indicates it was still under test. (Chris Booth)

THE DIESEL DEPOT

Old Oak Common

Sightings Snapshots

Saturday August 7, 1971

Class 08	3051/600/02/954/61/62/65/66/4003/25/166/77/79
Class 31	5530/35/36/39
Class 35	7026/8/30/33/45/48/52/53/66/81/100
Class 43	833
Class 47	1638/42/47/48/53/60/74/76/80/745
Class 52	1002/35/41

Saturday January 20, 1979

Class 08	08109, 08480, 08656, 08678, 08787, 08793, 08948
Class 31	31123, 31131, 31135, 31154, 31163, 31165, 31209, 31224, 31296, 31300, 31304, 31413
Class 47	47054, 47059, 47087, 47474, 47482, 47508
Class 50	50025, 50045

Saturday February 9, 1980

Class 08	08627, 08630, 08678, 08758, 08785, 08787, 08793, 08797, 08886, 08936, 08944, 08947, 08948
Class 31	31117, 31118, 31123, 31131, 31153, 31162, 31163, 31213, 31241, 31254, 31256, 31257, 31265, 31304, 31308, 31412, 31415
Class 47	47056, 47089, 47095, 47142, 47146, 47205, 47443, 47501
Class 50	50016, 50025, 50029, 50030, 50040

Wednesday December 29, 1982

Class 08	08480, 08651, 08781, 08797, 08821
Class 31	31118, 31158, 31165, 31273, 31286, 31294, 31304, 31307, 31326
Class 43	43138, 43152
Class 47	47030, 47056, 47068, 47076, 47083, 47096, 47129, 47152, 47186, 47363, 47484, 47486, 47508, 47509, 47512, 47536
Class 50	50012, 50017, 50045, 50050

Monday May 30, 1983

Class 08	08480, 08486, 08798, 08936, 08944, 08947
Class 31	31120, 31135, 31139, 31141, 31256, 31327
Class 43	43134
Class 47	47054, 47070, 47078, 47094, 47103, 47232, 47341, 47438, 47484, 47500, 47508, 47511, 47559
Class 50	50003, 50011, 50020, 50023, 50024, 50036, 50037

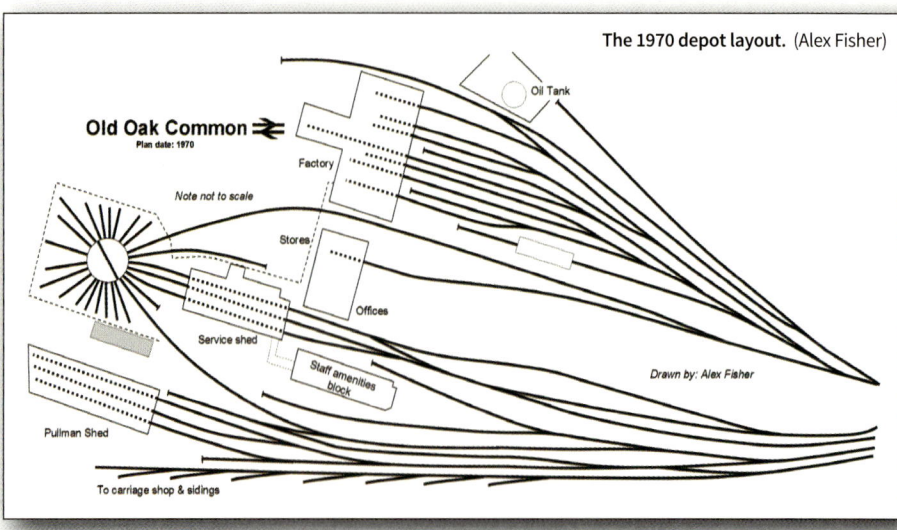

The 1970 depot layout. (Alex Fisher)

was disbanded in July 1991. In March 1995, the EWOC pool of Trainload Freight South London/West shunters based at Old Oak Common had nine diagrams covering the TMD, carriage sidings, Paddington, Reading, Cocklebury Yard, Swindon station, Didcot Yard, and Southall and Westbury Yard pilots. The EWOC pool used 36 Class 08s and 15 Class 09s between March 1994 and August 1999.

Hoovers, Guinness and Parcels

In May 1974, Class 50s D405 (50005) and 50001/2/4/50 were re-allocated to the shed from Crewe on the LMR. From June 1979 further Class 50s came, and ultimately 50021-40 and 50048 all saw allocations. The residency of 'Hoovers' at Old Oak lasted until July 1990 when 50023/4/6/35 were moved away.

From 1975 until 1998 there were 82 different Class 08s allocated to OC and 63 Class 31s. In March 1994, 09101 and 09102 were the first Class 09s to come and a total of 13 served through to 1998. In 1985 Guinness purchased two 08s (08022 and 08060) for use at its Park Royal establishment. The pair received the names *Lion* and *Unicorn* respectively and received maintenance at Old Oak along with locos from other depots, notably Laira Class 50s. From December 1987 to March 1991 former Class 25 97252 was based at OC and 97654, a departmental loco similar to a Class 04, resided from March 1994 until July 1996.

At the end of 1987 the Level 4 depot was home to nine HST sets, nine Class 08 shunters, five Class 31s, 25 Class 47s and 17 Class 50s. Reflecting the poor state of the Class 50s at the time, up to six of the class were usually on shed for repair at any one time. Into early 1991 the depot was maintaining Class 47s for BRs Intercity and Parcels sectors. Class 50s were also regular visitors, but by this time were being used on Waterloo to Exeter turns on the Southern. On June 5, 1991, 47847 became the first loco to undergo a power unit change at the depot. The Intercity long range fuel tank-equipped loco was a Crewe engine at the time. The last resident Class 47s left in March 1994.

Privatisation to closure

When privatisation came the depot buildings were taken over by EWS and were later run by its commercial subsidiary Axiom Rail. In October 1996, the 12 modified Class 37s for Eurostar (37601-12) arrived and 37601-6 were still resident in 1998 alongside two Class 73s (73118 and 73130) that had called the depot home since September 1997, as well as 14 Class 08s and eight Class 09s.

In 1997, a new bespoke depot to service and maintain the Heathrow Express (HEX) and Heathrow Connect service trains was built on the south side of the site beside the HST Depot. It was funded by BAA, thus making it the first new privately funded passenger train depot in the UK since nationalisation. When the Crossrail project received the go ahead, the depot and adjacent Coronation Carriage Sidings were fenced off in 2009 as they were to be compulsorily purchased. By mid-2011 the remaining GWR buildings and the Coronation Carriage Sidings had been demolished and the former western shed turntable had been donated to the Swanage Railway. The site was used temporarily to manufacture tunnel lining blocks for Crossrail, and now a new depot to maintain Crossrail EMUs is being built.

A trio of withdrawn Hymeks by the turntable on October 5, 1974. The large building immediately above them was the staff lodging building, where several footplatemen lived; it was also home to the Staff Association club. (Tom Connell)

MAGAZINE SPECIALS

ESSENTIAL READING FROM KEY PUBLISHING

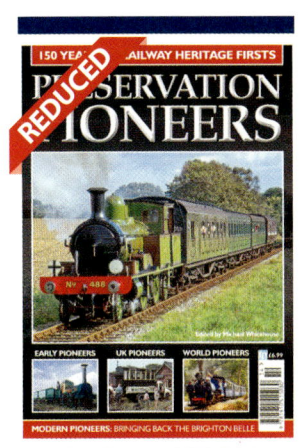

PRESERVATION PIONEERS
The story of those pioneering individuals, without whom there would not be heritage railways as we know them today.

£1.99 inc FREE P&P*

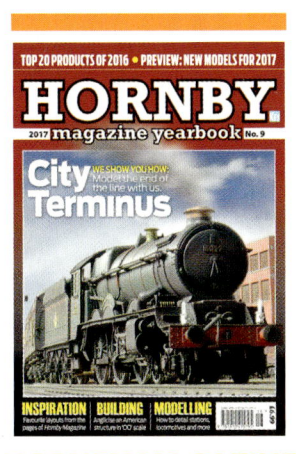

HORNBY MAGAZINE YEARBOOK 9
Hornby Magazine creates a 1960s Western Region style city terminus.

£6.99 inc FREE P&P*

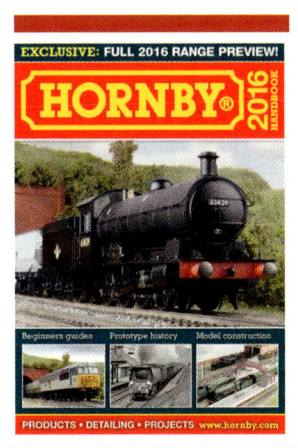

HORNBY HANDBOOK 2016
Bringing together full details on Hornby's 2016 range together with practical guides to railway modelling.

£7.99 inc FREE P&P*

HORNBY MAGAZINE YEARBOOK 8
This latest layout build by the Hornby Magazine team focusing on a 1980s period power station.

£3.99 inc FREE P&P*

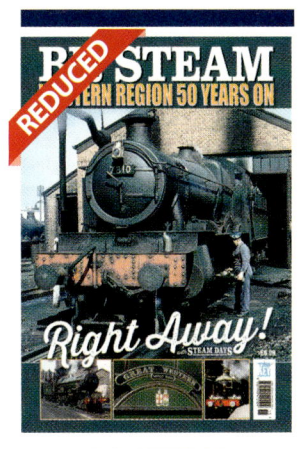

HORNBY MAGAZINE GREAT LAYOUTS
25 of the best layouts from the pages of Hornby Magazine.

£6.99 inc FREE P&P*

NARROW GAUGE STEAM
A celebration of the 150th anniversary of the introduction of steam on the Ffestiniog Railway.

£2.99 inc FREE P&P*

WEATHERING GUIDE
Covers all the tips and techniques you will need to develop your own weathered models.

£3.99 inc FREE P&P*

BR STEAM
Commemorates the 50th anniversary of the end of steam on British Railways Western Region.

£3.99 inc FREE P&P*

MAGAZINE SPECIALS
ESSENTIAL reading from the teams behind your FAVOURITE magazines

HOW TO ORDER

VISIT www.keypublishing.com/shop

OR

PHONE
UK: 01780 480404
ROW: (+44)1780 480404

*Prices correct at time of going to press. Free 2nd class P&P on all UK & BFPO orders. Overseas charges apply. Postage charges vary depending on total order value.

FREE Aviation Specials App
Simply download to purchase digital versions of your favourite aviation specials in one handy place! Once you have the app, you will be able to download new, out of print or archive specials for less than the cover price!

IN APP ISSUES **£3.99**

060/17

Eastfield

Eastfield

The Edinburgh to Glasgow railway began in 1842 and soon saw considerable growth in passengers and freight. The North British Railway (NBR) opened a new engine shed in September 1904 on a green-field site north of Springburn in Glasgow. Eastfield was the NBR's largest depot, capable of holding 84 locos at its 14-road shed. The depot was rebuilt after a fire in June 1919 and went on to have an allocation of roughly 200 steam engines. In February 1950, Eastfield became 65A, with several sub sheds including Aberfoyle (until 1951), Helensburgh (1960-1961), Kilsyth (until 1951), Kipps (1962), Lennoxtown (until 1951), Motherwell (from 1972), Parkhead (1962) and Polmadie (from 1972). Additionally, a further ten sheds came under 65A's control from 65B St Rollox to 65K Polmont, and included: 65F Grangemouth from 1950 to 1973 and Fort William as 65J from 1950 to 1970 and then 65H from 1970 to 1973.

From steam to diesel

The first diesel allocated to Eastfield Depot was the shunter (later Class 08) 13207 in January 1956. Subsequent months saw another six arrive, along with a single example of what was to become Class 12 (15229) in November 1958. As 15229 was a Southern-based engine at the time, it's doubtful whether it ever made it to Eastfield for the one month it was supposedly allocated there. On Sunday June 30, 1957 Eastfield held 98 engines, including 13207/9/10/12/14/15/16. Interestingly, 13207/9/10 were Eastfield machines, while 12212/14 were allocated to Parkhead and 13215/16 to St Rollox. The first main line loco diesel to be based at Eastfield was the wandering Brush Type 2 D5511, which had a short spell at the Scottish depot from June to July 1958. For November 1958 only, BRCW Type 2 D5303 had the briefest of spells there.

On Sunday June 1, 1958 there were 111 steam locomotives on shed, as well as 0-6-0 diesels D3133/207/11/388/9/90/91/93/96, 13209 and 13212.

At weekends during the 1970s and 80s the eastern end of the depot was guaranteed to be packed to the rafters with locos. This is the view on September 4, 1977, with 47038, 47119 and 47464 among the locos visible.
(Gavin Morrison)

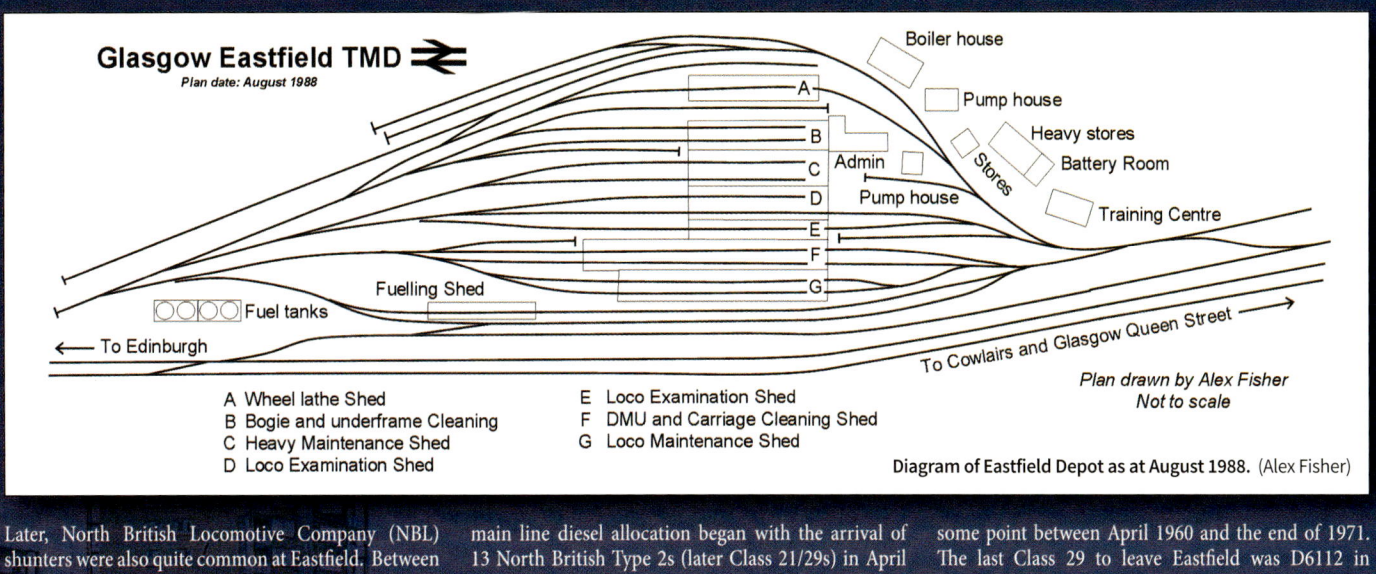

Eastfield

Glasgow Eastfield TMD
Plan date: August 1988

A Wheel lathe Shed
B Bogie and underframe Cleaning
C Heavy Maintenance Shed
D Loco Examination Shed
E Loco Examination Shed
F DMU and Carriage Cleaning Shed
G Loco Maintenance Shed

Plan drawn by Alex Fisher
Not to scale

Diagram of Eastfield Depot as at August 1988. (Alex Fisher)

Later, North British Locomotive Company (NBL) shunters were also quite common at Eastfield. Between May 1960, when the first one (D2757) arrived, and February 1968, when the last ones left, the depot had seen 33 different examples come and go. Eastfield's main line diesel allocation began with the arrival of 13 North British Type 2s (later Class 21/29s) in April 1960. Their ranks soon swelled and while D6152 had a brief spell at the depot in 1968, Eastfield was home to every example of the type from D6100 to D6137 at some point between April 1960 and the end of 1971. The last Class 29 to leave Eastfield was D6112 in December 1971.

Class 20s were also very prominent there and when D8070 arrived in June 1961 it marked the start of a long

THE DIESEL DEPOT | 41

Eastfield

Sightings Snapshots

August 5, 1964

0-6-0 shunter	D3416
EE Type 1	D8073/074/082/099/103/111/112
NBL Type 2	D6109/110/111/126/128/132/134/135/136
BRCW Type 2	D5349/361/365
EE Type 4	D361
D2/10 shunter	D2760/D2762/D2763/D2765/D2770

April 17, 1976

Class 08	08143, 08321, 08326, 08347, 08348, 08447, 08561, 08566, 08621, 08718, 08733, 08735, 08754, 08755, 08853, 08855
Class 20	20027, 20055, 20079, 20094, 20095, 20102, 20110, 20116, 20117, 20122, 20137
Class 24	24006, 24106, 24113, 24116
Class 25	25002, 25010, 25019, 25021, 25083, 25098, 25101, 25172, 25226, 25234
Class 26	26023, 26035
Class 27	27001, 27002, 27005, 27006, 27010, 27011, 27013, 27016, 27031, 27032, 27035, 27036, 27037, 27041, 27042, 27044, 27104, 27106, 27109, 27211
Class 37	37154, 37155, 37204, 37237
Class 40	40064
Class 47	47059, 47210, 47285, 47550

February 23, 1980

Class 08	08346, 08402, 08447, 08693, 08733, 08761
Class 20	20002, 20020, 20039, 20080, 20094, 20170
Class 24	24006
Class 25	25002, 25050, 25066, 25076, 25079, 25083, 25109, 25231, 25232, 25233, 25235, 25238, 25239, 25240
Class 27	27003, 27008, 27010, 27011, 27012, 27017, 27024, 27025, 27028, 27034, 27036, 27037, 27042, 27043, 27101, 27104, 27107, 27112, 27202, 27204, 27207, 27208, 27210, 27211
Class 37	37081, 37155, 37237
Class 40	40158, 40165
Class 47	47141, 47149, 47407, 47517

May 2, 1981

Class 08	08196, 08402, 08544, 08693, 08721, 08733, 08764, 08952
Class 20	20002, 20036, 20118, 20125, 20146, 20179
Class 25	25227, 25230, 25233, 25239, 25240, 25247, 25260
Class 26	26008, 26040
Class 27	27016, 27020, 27026, 27030, 27032, 27036, 27042, 27101, 27102, 27103, 27109, 27205, 27206
Class 37	37012, 37014, 37021, 37022, 37026, 37027, 37033, 37081, 37112, 37117, 37144, 37156, 37196
Class 40	40064, 40160
Class 47	47053, 47102, 47206

May 8, 1982

Class 08	08447, 08693, 08721, 08733, 08852, 08938, 08952
Class 20	20002, 20021, 20028, 20149, 20156, 20191
Class 25	25109, 25233, 25240
Class 26	26014
Class 27	27012, 27016, 27017, 27018, 27023, 27024, 27025, 27026, 27028, 27029, 27033, 27034, 27038, 27043, 27109, 27204, 27205, 27208, 27211
Class 37	37011, 37026, 37028, 37037, 37108, 37111, 37114, 37151, 37261
Class 40	40173
Class 47	47141, 47207, 47269, 47542, 47570
DMU	Sc51464, Sc51465, Sc51466, Sc51524, Sc51535, Sc51538, Sc51807, Sc59552, Sc59556, Sc59562, Sc59568

January 29, 1983

Class 08	08443, 08447, 08733, 08736, 08763, 08793, 08938, 08952
Class 20	20028, 20037, 20045, 20083, 20086, 20111, 20117, 20216, 20225
Class 27	27004, 27016, 27022, 27023, 27026, 27043, 27059, 27101, 27204, 27210
Class 37	37014, 37018, 37033, 37043, 37108, 37157, 37175, 37190, 37191, 37253, 37265
Class 47	47040, 47049, 47093, 47149, 47206, 47221, 47415, 47461, 47541, 47578
Heating units	ADB968001 (ex-D8233), ADB968009 (ex-24142)
DMU	Sc50823, Sc50829, Sc50836, Sc50876, Sc50877, Sc50879, Sc50892, Sc51451, Sc51455, Sc51458, Sc51518, Sc51534, Sc51537, Sc51538, Sc51800, Sc55015, Sc59027, Sc59337, Sc59347, Sc59354, Sc59545, Sc59559, Sc59687, Sc59690, Sc59692

September 18, 1985

Class 08	08343, 08348, 08793, 08852
Class 20	20125, 20137, 20198
Class 27	27010, 27014, 27022, 27043, 27045, 27207
Class 37	37026, 37036, 37056, 37085, 37175, 37190, 37263, 37402
Class 47	47018, 47120, 47595, 47701
Class 25	ADB97250 (ETHEL 1, ex-25310) ADB97252 (ETHEL 3, ex-25314)
DMU	Sc51453, Sc51518, Sc51526, Sc51536, Sc51537, Sc51797, Sc51798, Sc51802, Sc59554, Sc59555, Sc59564, Sc59691

Two ex-works Class 27s (27008 and 27115), together with Class 26 26046 at Eastfield on April 30, 1984. The three would have been recently overhauled at the nearby St Rollox Works. (Gavin Morrison)

association with the English Electric Type 1. Up to 1974 88 different examples called Eastfield home, including every one between D8070 and D8137. Eastfield shunter allocation grew to a vast collection of Class 08s, and by 1974 it had hosted 75 different examples.

As late as June 19, 1965 Eastfield was still home to seven steam locos and when St Rollox (65B) closed to steam its locos came to Eastfield on November 7, 1966, although on November 30 Eastfield itself closed to steam. However, steam locos occasionally visited the wheel drop after this date, with 76046 noted there in April 1967.

At the time most of Eastfield's diesels were in the Type 2 power range. The BRCW Type 2s (later Class 27s) came to Eastfield in 1961 and their large numbers made

42 THE DIESEL DEPOT
www.railwaysillustrated.co.uk

Eastfield

The western end of the depot was not photographed as often as the eastern end, but in this April 30, 1984 view, Class 20s 20089 and 20144 can be seen, with an ETHEL Class 25, a Class 37, a DMU and parts of the breakdown crane in the background. Ex-works 20144 had just emerged from St Rollox Works and was waiting to head to its home depot at Tinsley. (Gavin Morrison)

Newly converted ETH-equipped 37/4 37401 inside the fuelling bay at Eastfield on July 9, 1985, the day after it arrived from Crewe Works. (Gavin Morrison)

One of the Class 47/7s used for push-pull Glasgow to Edinburgh services, 47706, receives attention inside the maintenance depot at Eastfield on September 4, 1988. (Gavin Morrison)

up the backbone of the depot's diesel fleet throughout the 1960s and into the 1970s. Class 24s arrived at Eastfield in October 1966 (D5050-6). D5065 and D5066 followed in March 1968, but two months later they'd all been transferred away, mainly to Longsight in Manchester.

A weekend visit in September 1967 found steam engines 44796, 76098 and 80002 working as stationary boilers, alongside 85 diesels. Class 06s were also allocated to Eastfield and the first one (D2410) came in August 1967, followed by 29 other examples by the early 1970s. In June 1968, Class 40 D363 had a brief residency at the depot until May 1970 which, like most short-term single loco allocations, was probably for staff training purposes.

In the late 1960s the triangle of lines adjacent to the depot was used for dumping diesels. NBL locos were the most common, with D6105/10/5 added in July 1968 followed by D6110/1/52 by the August. In October 1968, 2-6-4T 80002 went onto the Eastfield dump and was replaced by an NBL Class 21 on carriage heating duties. On September 1, 1969, 12034/5, along with 2573 and 6111, were on the triangular dump. With steam finally banished, a portion of the steam shed furthest from the main line had been demolished by September 1968. Re-construction of the shed as a diesel depot soon started and by September 1969 the first steelwork was in place. At the turn of the decade, the newly opened diesel depot was seeing a wide variety of allocated and visiting locos, including the occasional Class 50.

The 1970s

Class 24s returned to Eastfield from March 1971 and by March 1972 every one from 24001 to 24019 had come to the depot. A further 20 examples followed, but in August 1975 all of those remaining were transferred away. Generally replacing them was a mass influx of Class 25s; July 1971 saw a trio (D5176/7/80) make the journey north in a move from Holbeck. By December 1976, 77 examples had been allocated to the depot; the same month saw 25301 became the last inward transfer of the class. In May 1971 a second Class 26 (D5329) came from Haymarket to Eastfield, but by August it had moved back – its brief spell perhaps being for crew training.

Under the TOPS system Eastfield's code became ED in May 1973. In May the next year a tranche of 17 Class 47s came and in July 1975 Eastfield had an allocation of 220 locos: 2 x 06, 31 x 08, 54 x 20, 36 x 24, 8 x 25, 57 x 27, 17 x 37, 15 x 47. The depot supplied the Class 27s used on the Glasgow to Edinburgh push-pull trains, but as the 27s' mechanical condition deteriorated they were replaced by specially modified Class 47/7s and rakes of Mk 3 coaches, with a driving trailer (DBSO) being introduced in December 1980.

A visit to the depot on Sunday July 15, 1979 found 64 locos on shed of classes 08, 24-27, 37, 40 and 47. 06002, Eastfield's last Class 06, left the depot in May 1979, while the facility retained its prolific allocation of Class 08s. Its shunter duties in 1979 were among the largest in Britain, with 21 diagrams. They included two at Whifflet Basin Sidings near Coatbridge, two at Yoker Sidings and one each at Greenock Ladyburn Yard, Shieldhall Wharf and Paisley Canal. There were seven in the Polmadie area and seven in the Eastfield area to cover Parkhead North Freight Depot, Cowlairs Carriage Sidings, St Rollox BREL Works pilot, Cadder Yard and Glasgow High Street Freight depot, as well as two at Sighthill Freight Depot.

The 1980s

Saturday February 23, 1980 found 61 locos at Eastfield from Classes 08, 20, 24, 25, 37, 40 and 47. Class 25s continued to be based here until October 1982, when the final dozen transferred away. Additional arriving Class 20s meant that many of the class had spent at least some time at Eastfield, even if several, such as 20006's stay from March to October 1982, were only brief. Most interestingly is the way the Class 37s went from only a small presence to being the most numerous class in the early 1980s. The second most numerous type at ED in the 1980s was the Class 47, and although many were

THE DIESEL DEPOT | 43

Eastfield

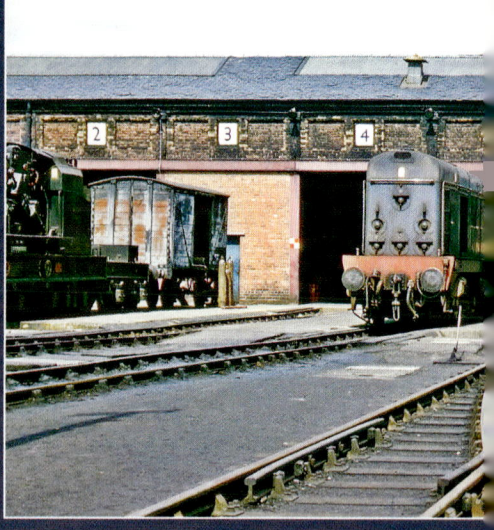

ABOVE LEFT: Eastfield was used to service DMUs for many years during BR days. This example is attended to on June 30, 1970. (Chris Booth)

ABOVE RIGHT: BRCW/Sulzer Type 2 D5368 is flanked by English Electric Type 1s D8090 and D8097 in front of the old steam shed at Eastfield on July 15, 1965. (Bill Wright)

there in the 1970s, it was the 1980s that really saw their numbers mushroom. Most notably, 47701-17 all came to Eastfield in October 1987, but by October 1990 they'd all left and in March 1991 the last few examples had also gone as the depot wound down for closure.

In April 1984 the depot had an allocation of 162: 14 x 08, 52 x 20, 97250-2, 32 x 27, 39 x 37 and 22 x 47. In May 1987 the mass migration of Class 26s to Eastfield began, and many more followed in 1988. It was around this time that the depot saw the end of its long association with the Class 27 when the final examples were moved away in July 1987. At the end of the 1980s the loco allocation was declining, but in November 1989 it still comprised 104 main line engines: 8 x 20, 30 x 26, 30 x 37, 36 x 47, but no Class 08s.

ETHELS and Scottie Dogs

When the London Midland Region started using Mk 3 sleepers, some Scottish lines could not accommodate ETH-fitted Class 47s due to route availability issues. Eastfield's steam heat-equipped Class 37s were still working the Fort William sleeper trains, so as a 'stop-gap' three withdrawn Class 25s were converted for use as mobile ETH sources known as Electric Train Heating Ex-Locomotive or 'ETHEL'. The three were 97250 (ex-25310), 97251 (ex-25305) and 97252 (ex-25314) and were allocated to Eastfield from June, August and July 1983 respectively. ETHEL 2 97251 was noted at ED on August 5, 1984 and was employed to provide ETH on routes where Class 47s were banned. Eventually, Crewe began releasing ETH-fitted Class 37/4s, and 37401 (ex-37268) arrived at Eastfield in late June 1985. Sufficient Class 37/4s had reached Eastfield by summer 1986 and the use of ETHELs was discontinued. 97252 was transferred away in October 1986, followed by 97250/1 in January the following year.

In the 1980s the depot was notable for applying a white Scottie Dog sticker to its locos; the emblem originated from publicity material for the West Highland line. When the Railfreight sub-sector aluminium diamonds were introduced, Eastfield naturally adopted the Scottie Dog on the cast plate. The diamonds were mainly applied to Railfreight traction, but Eastfield enthusiastically included them on passenger and infrastructure traction, too.

Demise and closure

Class 158 DMUs were introduced on the Glasgow to Edinburgh services in 1990 and their arrival exacerbated Eastfield's declining loco population. Class 26001 was turned out in Civil Engineers 'Dutch' livery and was later named *Eastfield* on July 26, 1991 at the depot. In February 1992 the proposed closure of Eastfield Depot sparked impassioned pleas for its retention from Michael J Martin, MP for Springburn Glasgow. As the Minister for Public Transport, Roger Freeman pointed out, however, in 1986 the diesel fleet in Scotland stood at 235,

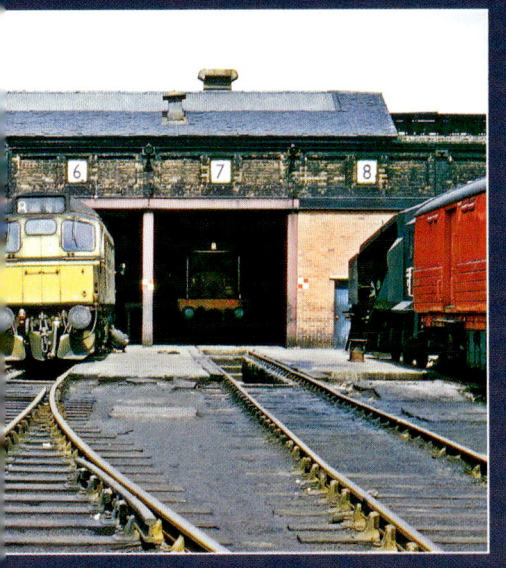

Eastfield

British Rail/Sulzer Type 2 D5006 on shed pilot duty at Glasgow Eastfield as construction of the new diesel depot goes on in the background on July 8, 1971. (Rail Photoprints/Ronald F Collen-Jones)

but in 1992 it was down to 98, with further reductions foreseen. He added that BR had reviewed Eastfield's position in 1991 and all BR's businesses were consulted, but no prospect of alternative extra work for the depot emerged. After careful consideration of long-term requirements, BR came to the conclusion that closure was the most cost-effective solution.

In mid-1992 an October date was mooted for the depot's closure and, in preparation, all of the Trainload Coal traction was moved to Motherwell Depot. At the time ED employed 120 people and the closure was expected to coincide with the shutting of British Steel's Ravenscraig plant. Staff were to be offered alternative employment and the depot's work was to be split between Ayr, Grangemouth, Inverness and Motherwell depots, the latter slightly offsetting some of its lost Metals Work. The diminishing requirement for locos in the Glasgow area was brought about by all-but-ending loco-hauled passenger trains and the decimation of freight traffic, which rendered the depot superfluous. On August 21, 1992, 26007 and 26001 were officially brought out of the shed in their newly applied green liveries for a short ceremony to mark the closure. Demolition soon followed, but that wasn't to be the end of a depot in the Eastfield area.

Privatisation and rebirth

Privatisation brought increased service levels and enhancements into the region's railways and the most prominent service was, and still is, the Glasgow to Edinburgh shuttles. ScotRail invested heavily in a fleet of new Bombardier Class 170 units and, in order to maintain them adequately, a new facility was opened near to the former Eastfield Diesel Depot site. Consultants White Young Green designed the earthworks profiles and drainage, along with the track layout and signalling for the depot.

The land had been used first by steam and then by diesels for 100 years and was heavily contaminated. Some 20,000m^3 of material had to be removed before 2.3km of new track and 4km of drainage could be installed. As the new depot was mainly to be used for carriage cleaning, elevated platforms totalling 800m were added, along with 5,000m^2 of external hard standing. By July 2004 the skeleton frame of the main depot building, which was a 14,000ft^2 two-road shed, had been erected and a start made on the fuelling building. In total the C Spencer-built depot cost £14m and today is used predominantly for servicing DMUs on the Glasgow to Edinburgh services. Funding for the project came from the Scottish Executive's Integrated Transport Fund and the new depot opened on December 13, 2004. Today it is used by DMU Classes 156/8/70, with the very occasional visit from a diesel or steam loco on a charter working.

Type 3 power as Class 37s dominate in this image taken on June 15, 1985. Identified are (l-r) 37037, 37085, 37027, 37263, 37178, with one unidentified example. (Gavin Morrison)

Toton

Toton's yards and steam depot were certainly impressive, but its diesel depot, claimed as being the largest in Western Europe when it opened, was even more remarkable.

Steam supreme

As 18A, Toton's extensive steam facilities in the 1950s included three roundhouses. No 1 shed was built by the Midland Railway (MR) in 1870, making it the oldest and smallest of the three. An 8F steam locomotive could only just fit on its turntable with an inch to spare at each end of its wheels. No 2 shed was bigger and also housed the driver's mess room and lockers. No 3 was the largest and housed the heavy machinery for maintenance, and was thus mostly used as a repair shop. In the 1930s Toton had a large mechanical coaling plant built that could lift whole wagons up and over to empty their contents into a bunker ready for direct filling into the awaiting steam engines underneath. Due to the amount of ash produced by Toton's large steam engine fleet, it also had a mechanical ash plant that would lift tubs of ash from the pits and empty them directly into wagons below.

Starting with shunters

Toton's very first diesel was London, Midland and Scottish Railway (LMS) shunter 1831. This wonderful looking machine was an experiment to create a diesel hydraulic shunter out of a rebuilt MR 1377 Class 0-6-0T steam loco of the same number. Originally built at Vulcan Foundry in September 1892, work to transform it was undertaken at Derby Works. The frames and running gear of the original were retained; the rebuilt loco being ready for trials in 1932. It came to Toton in May 1934, but as the experiment was deemed unsuccessful, it was put into storage in 1936 and officially withdrawn in

September 1939. It was then converted into a mobile power unit and emerged in its new guise as MPU3 in November the following year; scrapping eventually came in August 1951.

In May 1939, LMS shunter 7080, followed in June by 7082/3/4, all came to Toton. They were part of an order for 40 shunters built at Derby Works and utilised English Electric transmissions. They represented the depot's first foray into a diesel fleet, for which rudimentary facilities were provided. During World War Two further examples were brought to Toton, while ten of the 40 machines were sent to serve abroad. The 30 that remained were given numbers from 12003 to 12032 and in September 1945 Toton had 12006/7/8/12/32 on its books.

The shunters that were later to be assigned the BR Class 11 first came to Toton in May 1945 in the form of 7120 and 7121, but only for one month. On March 6, 1949 it had 139 locos on shed, 11 of which were diesels: 7084/5/125 and 12006/12/20/45/6/7/8/50. In the late 1940s 12038/45/7/56/7/8/ came to Toton and 1950 saw the addition of 12066/69/70/1/2/3. In June 1954 13056 became the first of what later became Class 08 to be allocated to the depot, although it only stayed until August 1956. From June 1955 Toton received 13117, the first of ten shunting engines that were part of a batch of Crossley-powered shunters similar to an '08'. Three more '08s' came in February 1957 – 13289/92/3.

Main line Mecca

The very first main line diesel for British Railways was Class 20 D8000, which arrived in August 1957. It only stayed one month before leaving, but it returned from June until September 1958. British Thomson-Houston Type 1 D8203 (later Class 15) was either loaned or allocated to Toton in March 1958 until May, followed in November 1958 by classmate D8208 until January 1959. In May 1959, BR/Sulzer Type 2 (later Class 24) D5008 came to Toton for a brief period, departing in September. On May 14, 1961 the depot held Metro-Vic Co-Bo D5714 along with Peak D80, 0-6-0s 12038/82, D3117/8/20/1/2/4/5/6/32/792 and 64 steam engines.

When DMUs came to Derby, those on the Crewe diagrams were serviced at Stoke's Cockshute Depot, while those used on the Lincoln route were attended to at Toton. With its Midland Railway Roundhouse, Toton wouldn't seem an obvious choice to service DMUs, but they used the long straight inspection pits down the inside of No 2 and No 3 roundhouses that had been specially constructed for the lengthy LMS Beyer-Garratt steam locos. This practice continued until the DMUs were transferred to Derby Etches Park in 1962.

The depot layout as in 1967. (Alex Fisher)

An image that typifies Toton during the 1970s and 80s in particular – long lines of work-stained Class 20s at weekends as they take a break from local coal traffic duties. Included in this line up on April 23, 1978 were 20006, 20041, 20113, 20157, 20167, 20171 and 20178. (Gavin Morrison)

Toton

ABOVE: Until the new diesel depot was built locos shared the old steam facilities. Immaculate BR/Sulzer Type 4 D57 contrasts with a filthy brake tender and equally dirty Standard 9F on July 14, 1963. (Rail Photoprints)

BELOW: Class 45/1s 45127 and 45150 undergo repairs inside the maintenance building in July 1985. Roads 14 and 15 had reinforced floors to allow the use of 20-ton electric screw lifting jacks. (Michael Rhodes)

In March 1962, BR Type 4 (late Class 44) D1 *Scafell Pike* came to Toton and by May 1962 all ten of the original Peaks were concentrated there. The class became synonymous with Toton until its withdrawal two decades later. Some of the class' first duties included taking over turns to Northampton, Birmingham and Wellingborough, and after Tinsley marshalling yard's opening they were a common sight on the evening freight there. This was on an out-and-back basis as only Toton men were trained on the type.

In anticipation of the mass influx of diesels that was to come, some of Toton's men were asked to be volunteer driver instructors on the new traction. An interesting nuance of the difference between steam and diesel was that the former had a natural braking affect when not under power thanks to the compression of the closed cylinders, whereas a diesel would carry on with freer momentum. This was one of the reasons why diesels needed brake tenders to cope with the braking of unfitted mineral trains. By the beginning of April 1962 at least seven green-liveried diesel brake tenders had been delivered to Toton and were being tested with BR/Sulzer Type 4s. They were later seen on trains descending the bank from Kirkby to Pinxton, and on other heavy unfitted mineral trains.

The first Class 46, D140 (46003), came to Toton in May 1962 and 16 different class members were allocated there in the 1960s. When BR/Sulzer Type 2 D5183 arrived in April 1963, it really marked the start of Toton's dieselisation. The type was used extensively on local colliery traffic, along with trips further afield to Corby's steelworks and Birmingham. In September 1963, Toton became 16A, but it should be noted that from January 1965 the London Midland Region (LMR) of BR started not allocating its locomotives to individual depots, but to more generic and larger pools based on divisions within its region. The LMR had several such divisions including: 'Nottingham' and 'Midland lines', and many of its locos were maintained and effectively based at Toton, albeit without an official allocation. In June 1963, D57 had been the first of what later became Class 45 allocated to Toton, and while many more joined it, they adopted the Divisional system. Notably the ten original Peaks, D1-10, and the 15 Brush Type 4s (Class 47), which had first come to Toton in August 1964, all went to the LMR Nottingham Division (D16) from January 1965.

Largest depot in Western Europe

The diesel fuelling area of the new depot opened first and two locos could be fuelled simultaneously from the 150,000-gallon fuel store. The servicing and light maintenance bays, roads 1-4, opened in November 1964; each had a 230ft pit over which three Type 4s could stand. The heavy maintenance section, roads 5-15, opened in February 1965 and each had a 154ft pit to be used for scheduled exams and unscheduled repairs. Importantly, each road only held two Type 4s and roads 5-14 had an elevated platform along half their length, with the depot floor below rail level in that area. Roads 13-15 had a 4-ton capacity overhead travelling crane for

BR/Sulzer Type 2s were synonymous with Toton from the early 1960s and were tasked with a wide range of mostly freight duties across the Midlands. Class 25/3 25260 stands outside the maintenance shed on April 4, 1981. (Rail Photoprints/John Chalcraft)

removing large equipment from locos, including steam heating boilers and generators.

In order to perform bogie changes and maintenance, roads 14 and 15 had specially reinforced concrete floors to support 20-ton electric screw lifting jacks. Two sets of jacks were used, one to lift bodies clear so the bogies and body underside could be cleaned at regular intervals, and the other for lifting locos for repair work. Roads 5-12 had a 1-ton capacity lifting crane over the elevated platform area only.

Other equipment included portable lubricant dispensers for new and used oil, compressed air-operated hand tools, steam heating boiler servicing equipment, welders, vacuum cleaners, floor cleaning machines, battery charging services and ultrasonic axle testing kit. Adjacent to the four through roads was the wheel profiling bay. It housed a ground wheel lathe that was able to re-profile loco or rolling stock wheels without removing them. Vehicles could be hauled into the bay and then positioned by capstans. It could also be used for loco road testing.

Locos entered the depot via hand- or electrically-operated folding doors and the whole building was centrally heated using waste oil to fire a boiler, while a ventilation system extracted diesel fumes. Unlike the dark dingy environs of steam depots, Toton was designed to make as much use of natural light as possible, supplemented by florescent tubular lighting in the pits.

At the dead end part of the shed the platforms were joined together to form a working area. To accommodate the large number of people working at Toton there was a well-equipped amenities block for 70 supervisory and clerical staff, along with 440 workshop men. There were facilities for signing on and off duty as well as a fully equipped classroom where the training of both maintenance staff and train crews was undertaken. Special workshops were provided for the plant and machinery staff and their apprentices. Additional rooms within the depot included those for maintenance of batteries, air panel filters, oil filters and injectors, together with testing of lubricating oil samples. Toton was built for the heavy maintenance and servicing of approximately 400 main line and 50 shunting locos used by the LMR. In total the depot could hold 34 Type 4s.

The first manager of Toton's new diesel depot was J V McKeating; his assistant was E E Bell and there were two operations supervisors. The senior foreman was called 'Shift Running Foreman Grade C', while the junior man was the 'Shift Running Foreman Grade B'. These names were later changed to a 'Train Crew Supervisor' and 'Traction Arranger'. The names were self-explanatory and the former arranged the train crews booking on and

ABOVE: By 1985 the Peaks were almost gone from Toton; however, in July 45056 shares the maintenance building with 56059 and 58010. (Michael Rhodes)

BELOW: Class 20s 20163 and 20170 are joined by 58017 in the maintenance building in July 1988. (Michael Rhodes)

An unidentified Class 56 and Peak 45108 stand on one of the refuelling roads on April 17, 1979. (Rail Photoprints/John Chalcraft)

Toton

ABOVE: Almost new English Electric Type 1 D8158 heads two other recently delivered examples at Toton in October 1966; the loco was delivered on September 2. (Colour-Rail)

BELOW: A cross section of the most prolific types at Toton is illustrated in this photo taken on July 11, 1976. From right to left are 25267, 44008 *Penyghent*, 47320 and 20197. (Gavin Morrison)

Toton diesel depot on March 28, 1965, barely two months after the facility fully opened. BR/Sulzer Types 2s dominate the scene, along with a couple of Brush Type 4s. The cleanliness compared with the old steam depot is obvious. (Bill Wright)

off along with covering shortages and general running matters. The latter dealt with the arriving locos and their fuelling and any further arrangements they required.

Locos arriving on depot would proceed to a sign that said "drivers must stop and report any defect at this point by telephone to the Traction Arranger". The driver would then be advised which fuel road to put the loco on. Those requiring further maintenance were advised to run onto No 1 fuel road, while those for return to traffic were to use No 2 road.

The former MR lodging house at Toton was closed in 1966, its 20 rooms no longer needed thanks to faster trains and a re-organisation of rosters to remove lodging; it was demolished sometime around 1973. One odd allocation to Toton was BR 0-6-0 shunter D2116 from October 1966 to September 1967 (withdrawn from Barrow-in-Furness in 1971). It was the only locomotive of its type ever allocated to the depot and with no others in the area or any obvious special need for it, this allocation is a mystery. Another example of a single type allocated to Toton was shunter D4106 (later 09018) from August until October 1968.

Although Brush Type 2s had workings from Wath Yard and the North Nottinghamshire Coalfield area that brought them into Toton's yards throughout the 1960s, only D5593 and D5694 were on the books and even then only for a month each in May 1973 and February 1974 respectively. Class 37s were similar to the 31s in that they had workings to Toton, again from the Eastern Region's Shirebrook area, but they weren't allocated there. The examples of D6774 in May 1973 and then D6835 in February 1974, the same singular months as the Class 31s, suggests they were there for crew training as a result of changed working practices.

Toton Allocations

Year	Total
1950	155 (Diesel Shunters not included)
1955	146
1960	118
1971	356 Toton 16A and Nottingham Division D16
1981	253
1988	278
1994	149
1998	207

Toton

ABOVE: Four class 20s (20088, 20097, 20139 and 20197), a Class 47 and a Peak rest at the north end of the depot on July 11, 1976. (Gavin Morrison)

BELOW: Peak 45133 raised up on jacks inside the maintenance building on April 20, 1984. (Gavin Morrison)

Diesels concentrated at Toton

In May 1973 the LMR practice of allocating locos to Divisions ceased and Toton became TO under the TOPS depot coding system. Twenty-three Class 47s within the number range D1630-D1960 went there and all of the Class 44s were formally allocated to the facility, although they had effectively been based there for 11 years. Every Class 45 except D12 and D14-7 had spent some part of the period 1965 to 1973 with the LMR Nottingham Division, while 88 of the 127-strong class were also assigned to Toton at some point during those years. Most importantly, May 1973 also saw the massive paper

Toton 1998 Allocation	
Class 08	08441/92/5/511/6/28/9/38/80/706/52/88 6/921
Class 37	37010/2/3/23/38/42/51/5/7/73/9/95/114/6/ 33/46/54/58/85/91/96/216/20/30/38/ 48/55 /8/62/332/79/403/23/31/503/19/677/80/706 /15/98/898/9
Class 58	58001-50
Class 60	60001-100
Class 66	66001

Another type that was synonymous with Toton was the BR/Sulzer Type original Peak, later to become Class 44 under TOPS. Number 44008 *Penyghent* (minus its nameplates) stands on the fuelling point on June 7, 1976. (Gavin Morrison)

THE DIESEL DEPOT 51

Toton

Sightings Snapshots

July 4, 1965 (plus 32 steam locos)

0-6-0 shunter	D3117/9/20/1/5/3696, 12035/8
BR/Sulzer Type 2	D5200/1/4/24/9/38/44/56/69/71/2/80, D7509/11/21/6/31/3/5/8/44/6/8/74/8
BR/Sulzer Type 2	D5394
BR/Sulzer Type 4	D1/2/3/4/5/7/8/9
BR/Sulzer Type 4	D10/2/30/7/8/51/6/7/62/5/74/84/95/102/8/10/8/21/8/32/6
BR/Sulzer Type 4	D147/9/51/8/62
Brush Type 4	D1623/5/6/8/30, D1809/12/6/8/21/6/30

January 2, 1971

0-6-0 shunter	3026, 3044, 3090, 3340, 3514, 3996, 3997
EE Type 1	8003, 8015, 8037, 8057, 8042, 8066, 8067, 8072, 8115, 8121, 8133, 8139, 8141, 8144, 8157, 8158, 8159, 8160, 8169, 8175, 8176, 8179, 8181, 8182, 8183, 8186, 8192, 8198, 8199, 8153, 8140, 8165, 8195
BR/Sulzer Type 2	5251, 5270, 7502, 7507, 7510, 7513, 7514, 7520, 7530
Brush Type 2	5809, 5827
EE Type 3	6821, 6829

BR/Sulzer Type 4	1/2/3/4/6/7/8/9/10
BR/Sulzer Type 4	29/42/3/6/8/55/6/62/7/72/6/7/82/103/16/27/128
BR/Sulzer Type 4	145/163
Brush Type 4	1623, 1716, 1802, 1805, 1816, 1823, 1825, 1839, 1941

February 24, 1979

Class 08	08018, 08021, 08027, 08181, 08292, 08334, 08398, 08399, 08536, 08741, 08829, 08858
Class, 20	20030, 20041, 20045, 20050, 20066, 20068, 20070, 20071, 20072, 20073, 20075, 20076, 20082, 20087, 20088, 20090, 20113, 20134, 20139, 20143, 20148, 20151, 20154, 20162, 20163, 20166, 20169, 20182, 20183, 20187, 20189, 20199
Class, 25	25127, 25129, 25221, 25242, 25262, 25283, 25303, 25316, 25318
Class 37	37132
Class 40	40135
Class 44	44004, 44007, 44009
Class 45	45005, 45044, 45050, 45051, 45056, 45059, 45062, 45073, 45105, 45107, 45117, 45122, 45136, 45144, 45150

Class 47	47306, 47321, 47334, 47365
Class 56	56036, 56037, 56038, 56039, 56040

June 17, 1984

Class 08	08019, 08320, 08597, 08666, 08741, 08757, 08829, 08858, 08899
Class, 20	20016, 20113, 20160, 20161, 20164, 20174, 20179, 20184, 20193, 20195, 20198, 20199, 20216, 20226
Class, 25	25257, 97202
Class31	31113, 31127, 31143, 31226
Class, 37	37187
Class, 45	45003, 45010, 45015, 45016, 45064, 45074, 45075, 45077, 45109, 45111, 45112, 45115, 45116, 45117, 45123, 45135, 45136, 45145, 45148, 45149
Class, 46	46009, 46023
Class, 47	47201, 47229, 47308, 47339, 47358, 47367, 47442, 47445, 47531
Class, 56	56058, 56059, 56064, 56066, 56067, 56068, 56069, 56071, 56072, 56074, 56084, 56116
Class, 58	58001, 58002, 58003, 58004, 58005, 58007, 58008, 58009, 58010, 58013
Class 15	ADB968002 (D8237)

move of 110 Class 20s onto Toton's allocation, along with a substantial number of Class 25s.

Terrific Toton
In October 1970 the depot received fuel oil via the 6D33 0623 SO Stanlow to Toton, and around that time an incredible number of locos arrived at and departed the shed. Often 60 or more would be disposed of in a single shift. A possible record is 95 that were stabled there one New Year's Eve in the early 1970s. Such were the numbers that weekends and bank holidays would see them stable on the Old Bank on roads 1-3.

Throughout the 1960s and 1970s Toton wasn't the freight-only depot it's often thought to have been. It played a vital role in maintaining the Midland Main Line's Class 45 fleet. The problem, however, was that their passenger services didn't actually take them past the depot. Thus to ensure these locos were swapped between Leicester, Derby and Nottingham as required, a special group of driving turns were introduced known as 'ferry turns'. These movements were to take rafts of locos between the depots and stations and there were five sign-on times per day for crews to ensure those made ready from the morning, afternoon and evening shifts were available for traffic as soon as possible.

Changing classes
Hump shunting of the down yard ceased in 1978 and all traffic requiring hump shunting was transferred to the up yard. In May 1977, 56031 was allocated to Toton from new, and in early 1979 Saltley was noted as hosting Class 56s that had worked from Toton to Didcot Power Station. The new Type 5s accelerated the move towards Merry-go-Round working and thus a reduction in the lower powered classes on the yard's books. Between 1974 and 1990, all bar a handful of Class 20s had spent at least some time allocated to Toton. The eight Class 20/3s were also based there until mid-1986.

Toton was home to 118 different Class 25s over the years, until 25096 was withdrawn on February 13, 1983 thus ending the class's permanent association, but not its residence. For example, 25151 (as 97202) had been acquired in October 1982 for re-railing exercises and managed to linger until August 1988. As the Class 25s had been run down, increasing numbers of Class 31s came and January 1983 saw some former Western Region examples arrive. After the release of new Type 5 58001 from Doncaster Works and its allocation to Toton in February 1983, the other 49 class members followed it, culminating with the arrival of 58050 in May 1985.

The 1980s rationalisation
Despite the MGR revolution resulting in the up yard closing for hump shunting in 1984, the depot was in

A general view of the northern side of the depot taken from the A52 road bridge in July 1988. (Michael Rhodes)

52 THE DIESEL DEPOT   www.railwaysillustrated.co.uk

Toton

ABOVE: Rays of afternoon sun help illuminate 47540 and Peak 45062 on July 17, 1978. (Gavin Morrison)

BELOW: Class 58 58037 receives attention within the depot on July 28, 1997. The raised platforms and the Class 58's access doors certainly made maintenance of the type much easier. (Gavin Morrison)

The GM invasion was underway at Toton on August 29, 1998 following the arrival of newly-built 66003, 66004 and 66005 for EWS. (Colour-Rail)

a healthy state. Maintenance staff numbers stood at around 360 in early 1983, with between 85 and 100 on the premises at any one time. However, in May 1986, BR announced major job losses and closures of depots and workshops, with Toton's wagon shops on the hit list.

On January 19, 1987 Toton became part of the Coal sub sector of Trainload Freight. As part of the change to even greater sectorisation, Speedlink traffic was diverted from there that January and concentrated on Derby St Mary's. However, Speedlink coal remained and at the same time a new flow started from Blidworth Colliery. In November 1986 Toton's association with Class 45s came to an end when its 62 examples were transferred to Tinsley, although a large number of withdrawn Peaks were still at the depot.

The LMR was recording a loco availability figure of 76% in April 1987 and as part of move towards sectorisation of assets, Toton's allocation of passenger and mixed traffic locos was transferred away in mid- to late-1987, which left the depot with 235: 98 Class 20s, 87 Class 56s and all 50 Class 58s. In mid-1987 Toton had Class 56s 56002-30/42/4/7/54/65-99, 56100/11 assigned for traffic from Tibshelf, Barrow Hill, Doncaster, Healey Mills, Knottingley, Shirebrook, Tinsley, Worksop and Blyth-Ellesmere Port. Of these, 28 (56002-29) moved to Toton in September 1986, while 56030/71-92 went in November and finally 56093-56111 in January 1987. A-exams continued to be carried out at Barrow Hill, Healey Mills and Doncaster, while B-exams could be undertaken at Shirebrook, Tinsley and Knottingley, and C-exams and above were performed at Toton. Ultimately, every single Class 56 except 56001 spent some time allocated to Toton in that time period.

Throughout the 1980s Toton continued to lose traffic. Losses included the closure of West Hallam Disposal Point, a reduction in production from the Stanton Gate complex, cessation of Speedlink services to the Metal Box factory at Kirkby-in-Ashfield and, most tellingly, the post-miners' strike loss of many local coal trains. Wagon load traffic returned to Toton in 1989 when Derby St Mary's closed on July 10, although during this time Speedlink traffic to Ollerton and Maltby collieries was lost. Countering this there were new Speedlink coal flows to Doncaster and Grimethorpe introduced in the November of 1989.

Toton's Indian Summer

Such was the contraction in traffic in the late 1980s that the smaller diesel depots in the East Midlands were closed. Westhouses was shut in 1987, by then merely

THE DIESEL DEPOT 53

Toton

An aerial view of Toton in April 2009, with large numbers of stored DB Schenker Class 60s evident. (Andy Martin)

a signing-on point in Tibshelf Sidings. And while a few drivers transferred to Toton, it took over the trips to Silverhill, Sutton and Bentinck collieries along with the residual traffic for Doe Hill oil terminal. Coalville closed in 1990, with Toton gaining trips to Lounge Disposal Point, Coalfields Farm and Drakelow Power Station. Derby and Nottingham train crew depots lost their Trainload coal turns to Toton and in February 1991, Shirebrook and Barrow Hill train crew depots were closed, with the bulk of their staff transferring to a new combined depot at Worksop. Shirebrook continued to serve as a fuelling point until September 27, 1996.

With locos and crews based at Worksop and Toton, the emphasis on train running centred on the base load power stations. Toton gained some of Barrow Hill's and Shirebrook's work, which had headed for the southern power stations at Didcot, Rugeley, Willington, Castle Donington, Drakelow, Staythorpe and Ratcliffe, while services to the northern power stations at Cottam, West Burton, Drax, etc were concentrated on Worksop. Toton's grip on the ex-Shirebrook jobs increased in the early 1990s as its drivers learned routes along the ex-Lancashire Derbyshire and East Coast railway to the collieries at Welbeck, Clipstone, Bilsthorpe, Thoresby and Ollerton. In addition to these, traffic also included coal for the stacking site at Rufford, trains from the Doe Hill open cast site and coal for High Marnham Power Station, all of which were shared with Worksop depending upon where the flows originated and where they were destined to go.

Toton still commanded large numbers of locos and on December 28, 1992 there were no fewer than 34 Class 20s there, along with recently introduced Class 60s 6000 3/10/32/7/58/68/73/4/8/79/89/90/3, which often pitched BR's oldest and newest locos side by side. In early 1993, Toton began undertaking CEM overhauls in order to avoid sending its locos to main works, and in April 1993, 56062 was the depot's second CEM overhaul.

1990s decline and privatisation

The announcement of mass colliery closures in 1992 hastened Toton's decline and reduced the requirement

A panoramic view of the packed depot on February 23, 1985. (Tom Connell)

54 THE DIESEL DEPOT
www.railwaysillustrated.co.uk

To mark the end of Class 47 use on cross country services a special line up of the regularly used Virgin locos, all wearing special liveries, was held at Toton on August 19, 2002. Instrumental in organising the occasion was EWS's Andy Lickfold. (Gavin Morrison)

for its fleet considerably. As privatisation loomed, it had around 170 drivers and it became part of Trainload Freight South-East, which soon became 'Mainline', with Toton as its HQ. English, Welsh & Scottish Railway (EWS) later bought the other two freight companies, Loadhaul and Transrail, along with RES and RfD, and Toton was chosen as the HQ and main depot. The facility held an open day on June 9, 1979 with more than 90 locos in attendance; EWS held a similar event in 1998. The new freight company invested heavily in order to be able to undertake all of its overhauling and maintenance work in-house. It built a new paint shop and an extension of the depot called 'the Cathedral', which contained a crane capable of lifting a power unit for exchanging and repairs without the loco having to visit a main works.

GM Invasion

In 1998 the first of 250 new General Motors/EMD Class 66s began arriving, leading to the demise of Toton's Class 31s, 37s and 47s, but, more tellingly, the traffic for which they were bought was either disappearing through closures or increasingly lost to Freightliner and other new entrants in the freight market. By 2000 Toton's trip workings were dwindling away and some of the remaining trains included the 6T93 1100 Toton to Oxcroft, the 7Z93 1300 Oxcroft to Healey Mills (which came back to Toton as the 6Z25 2215 Healey Mills to Toton), and the 6T38 0445 Toton to Welbeck and 7Z38 0730 Welbeck to Drakelow with the rake working back to Toton later. There were also trips from Stanton Gate, Chaddesden ballast tip and Ratcliffe with coal from Thoresby and Welbeck.

With little work for the 250 Class 66s, Toton's Class 58s and 60s were withdrawn in increasing numbers until the 58s were all stood down. With so little traffic and the economic downturn at the end of the 2000s, DB Schenker (which acquired EWS in 2007) closed both the Toton Old Bank and Toton New Bank yards on April 26, 2009. From then onwards all traffic was concentrated on Toton North Yard on the down side of the main line. In October 2009, the Erewash South re-signalling scheme was completed and control of the lines was passed from Trent Power Signal Box to the new East Midlands Control Centre at Derby. These changes also saw the closure of Stapleford and the Sandiacre shunt frame signal box, which was demolished at the start of 2011. Trains from Toton Depot and Toton North Yard can now run directly south along the bi-directional line on the down side, before using a new crossover near the old Long Eaton town station in order to access the up line.

The main use for the depot is the virtual quarry site behind, on the former down yard. The 800m-long site deals with 1.5m tonnes of railway ballast every year. It handles 1,700 tonne capacity trains delivering new ballast and processes 750,000 tonnes per annum of used ballast. New ballast comes from the Lafarge Mountsorrel quarry near Leicester for redistribution as far afield as Doncaster, Birmingham and Melton Mowbray.

Toton Today

Toton lost its Daw Mill Colliery to Ratcliffe services to GB Railfreight around 2005 and this left only occasional coal trains from Thoresby, Welbeck and opencast sites in Scotland. Trains of imported coal from Liverpool docks, Immingham and Avonmouth, and Network Rail ballast services from the nearby virtual quarry made up the remaining traffic. In mid-2010, DBS started to use the Old Bank sidings to stable coal trains from Daw Mill, which were heading for Ratcliffe. The New Bank sidings also saw occasional use, but by that time trees and bushes had become established, meaning some of the roads were unusable. In late April 2012 contractors were used to bring some of the New Bank sidings back into use for the stabling of the Network Rail Track Renewal System Train and the High Output Ballast Cleaning Train, which are seeing extensive use on the Midland Main Line and East Midlands area.

The most notable residents of the New Bank are the stored Class 60s, which have literally littered the yard for the last few years. The depot only had 48 drivers in 2010 and today it clings to life as DB Cargo's main repair and maintenance facility. The weekend ballast work and a few services to Ratcliffe are all that remain for a depot that once claimed to be Western Europe's largest.

What Depots Do

Large Logo liveried Class 56 56110 stands on the refuelling bay at Thornaby TMD in the company of some Class 08 shunters on March 16, 1985. At the time Thornaby was a Level 4 depot, capable of performing E-exams. (Rail Photoprints/Gordon Edgar)

WHAT DEPOTS DO

A depot's raison d'être is to ensure that its locomotive allocation meets its availability target and from the earliest days of diesels it was recognised that over periods of time different levels of work would be required. Early shunters were examined on a time-based interval system that went up to several years. This evolved into hours in service, but that didn't take into account the actual number of hours an engine was in use. Work varied quite considerably, even within the same class; turns and duties were different, which meant that some were put under far more strain than others. Thus examination intervals became ever more targeted to individual duties. Today each operator tailors its maintenance schedules and requirements to its fleet's characteristics and what is expected from it.

In the early years of diesel locomotives they had to make do with whatever facilities the incumbent steam shed had. At the most basic level a pit between the rails sufficed, but for larger examinations better access was required. New depots tended to include a three-level platform system, which was preferable, as the pits gave access under the bogies while the elevated track gave a better working height to the bogies. Finally, platforms gave cab-level access and, in the case of the Class 20s, access to the bodyside doors.

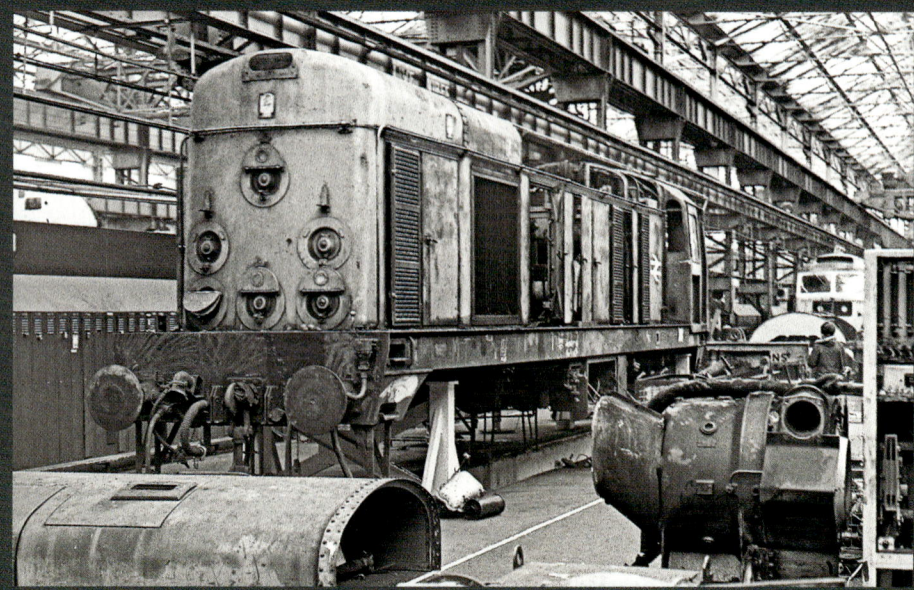

Major repairs and overhauls were performed by BR's works. Class 20 20097 undergoes a thorough strip down at Crewe Works on January 27, 1980. (Rail Photoprints)

THE DIESEL DEPOT

www.railwaysillustrated.co.uk

What Depots Do

Streamlining practices

With steam all but eradicated from BR by the end of the 1960s, its diesel fleet was experiencing better reliability and availability. The most important reason for the improvement was cleanliness. Even 15 or more years after the LMS had opened its dedicated diesel loco repair shop at Derby and noted that cleanliness was paramount, some BR regions had to learn it the hard way. The London Midland Region (LMR) seemed particularly stingy in the provision of diesel-only facilities and diesels on shed amongst steam locos were a common sight throughout the first half of the 1960s. A second point was that in 1962 the management of all railway workshops was transferred from the regions to a unified maintenance and repair organisation directly reasonable to the British Transport Commission (British Railways Board from 1963).

The central maintenance organisation was later named British Railways Workshops; and it became, in effect, a board of management with status equivalent to that of the BR regional management. The subsequent 1962 plan for BR's Workshops was one of a reducing requirement and a proposed closure of 15 out of 31, with a resultant decrease in staff numbers from 60,000 to 35,500. Ultimately, after modernisation and some £17m of expenditure, the remaining 16 primary works became British Rail Engineering Limited (BREL), which was incorporated on October 31, 1969. This second act created a distinct two-tier system of loco maintenance.

Periodic running maintenance, minor inspection and fault rectification were the responsibility of the Regional Chief Mechanical Engineer through his own regional depots, with major inspections and repairs involving extensive stripping becoming almost the sole responsibility of the independent workshop organisation – BREL. In fact, such was the difference in maintenance requirements of the new diesels, in August 1962 the railway unions were informed that with the swift elimination of steam power on BR, 19,000 workshop staff would be made redundant over the next five years.

Financial considerations

Particularly significant was the under-provision of a specialised maintenance and repair organisation. Such an approach is hard to fathom when the difference between costs for new diesels and their steam counterparts in the late 1950s was so startling. Steam locos ranged in price from as low as £14,627 for a 2-6-2T through to £20,000 or higher for a 4-6-2 and up to £33,497 for a 2-10-0 9F. Diesels, however, ranged in price quite considerably, with an English Electric Type 1 costing £58,955 through to a BR/Sulzer Type 4 costing £144,422, although the much more numerous EE Type 4 cost 'only' £106,807. By the end of 1963 BR had spent roughly £150m on new diesels.

Reports from the early 1960s lay clear the deficiencies of some of the early main line types, especially in-service failures and high rates of unreliability. In the early diesel years BR garnered only negligible advantages and economies but in 1963, and nearly a decade after their introduction, BR produced a report that showed the economies inherent in main line diesels were not just a chimera.

March Depot in East Anglia could perform B-exams and was primarily a servicing depot with a considerable allocation of Classes 31 and 37, including 37051 depicted here. (Michael Rhodes)

Servicing provision

The issue of provisions for servicing and maintenance is one on which the BR regions had stark differences of opinion. On the WR and ER especially, servicing and maintenance were seen as firmly separate functions, with Tinsley having its servicing shed down in the yard complex far away from the main depot. At Old Oak Common a similar situation purveyed, although they were much closer together. Conversely, on the LMR, Toton sited the fuelling, servicing and maintenance activities alongside each other, but Derby 4, Nottingham, Westhouses, Coalville and Burton sheds were poorly equipped. As a result Toton saw considerable congestion and difficulties at what was supposed to be one of Europe's premier depots.

Also evident in this period was that, compared to steam sheds, diesel depots had become an increasingly sophisticated and well-equipped resource. The aim was to keep each loco in service for the maximum amount of time between major exams, which were to be undertaken at main works. Consequently, repairs that once would have called for main works attention were now being achieved at depot level, thanks to the main works supplying depots with reconditioned parts under a component exchange system. The depots themselves were also better equipped, due to a programme of providing them with cranes and pit lathes, which meant fewer trips to works for wheel turning.

Efficiency

Diesel depots need far fewer men, no cleaners, boilermen or coaling staff, and their faster, more productive operation reduces the need for re-manning and lodging. The GE section of the Eastern, for example, soon achieved a ratio of 3.1 crew to 1 locomotive, against an ideal of 3 to 1. With steam a crew was averaging a mere 76 mile per turn of duty, but with diesels it rose to 124, with an average rostered time in movement of four hours 40 minutes per turn. Economy gains expanded almost in proportion to the growth of staff familiarisation with the new locos. New techniques and tools were developed as well, but perhaps most importantly, in 1966 Mr G T Smithyman, BR's first CME, helped the BRB to develop standardised maintenance schedules. In collaboration with the regional CMEs, he'd collated and pooled the knowledge and experience that existed around the regions, much to the benefit of BR's diesel fleet.

Finally, while traffic losses and line closures accounted for some of the reduction, the changeover from steam to diesel reduced loco numbers by 75% and many motive power depots were closed. By the end of 1966 all of the major depots were built or were soon to be opened, even if in most cases it was several years after the diesels had come to their respective areas. Vividly apparent, however, was the lack of clear and rigid guidance from the BR board that meant the regions were free to pursue different approaches to the styling and composition of maintenance and servicing depots.

Maintaining the diesels

While a steam engine required coal, water, oiling, its smoke box cleaning out and its fire tending whenever it visited its shed, a diesel needed a more rigorous schedule of checks and tests. Depending upon its diagram, a daily or two-day check would involve fuelling, testing its oils and coolants, and visual checks for leaks and breakages, or damage that could lead to a crew failing it. These checks and servicing could be done at a basic depot without even a covered road.

The Western Region, with its fleet of diesel hydraulics, had laid its depots out so that they could undertake unit replacement of almost all a loco's main parts within the confines of the depot. The quick-running engines of diesel hydraulics were lighter and a 10-ton crane could lift them out for exchange, which is why the WR's depots at Canton, Landore and Laira etc, had high buildings for the removal of such items, whereas most other depots on BR, which looked after mainly diesel electric, had lower roofs and relied upon main works for the removal and replacement of engines and generator assemblies. At Tinsley on the ER and Toton on the LMR, however, there was only a 1-ton capacity crane, despite each being their region's premier shed, as the largest activity undertaken was changing cylinder liner seals.

In early 1987 BR undertook a rationalisation of its loco and coaching stock maintenance policy. It classified each of its depots from Level 0, those that provided almost no maintenance capability (such as stabling points), through to Level 6, based upon their capabilities and available facilities. Level 1 was the fuelling point, which could also provide mainly unskilled staff for fuelling, oil and watering diesels, along with performing A-exams. A Level 2 depot could do up to a B-exam, while a Level 3 depot had facilities for D-exams, along with capabilities for maintenance and minor repair work. Up to an E-exam could be done at a Level 4 depot, while a Level 5 depot could carry out component exchange and maintenance overhauls up to an F-exam. Finally, Level 6 facilities were actually main works where full rebuilds and major collision damage were undertaken.

Level/Exam capability at BR Depots in the late 1980s	
1/A	Birkenhead North, Barrow-in-Furness, Chester, Corkerhill, Cricklewood, Exeter St Davids, Fratton, Fort William, Holyhead, Ipswich, King's Lynn, Newton Heath, Peterborough Nene Sidings, Perth, Saltley
2/B	Aberdeen Ferryhill, Ashford Chart Leacon, Allerton, Ayr, Brighton, Blyth Cambois, Bournemouth West, Buxton, Bletchley, St Blazey, Cambridge, Doncaster, Frodingham, Gateshead, Gloucester, Grangemouth, Healey Mills, Holbeck, Ilford, Kingmoor, Knottingley, Landore, Longsight, Leicester, Margam, March, Norwich Crown Point, Peterborough, Polmadie, Penzance, Reading, Ripple Lane, Shirebrook, Springs Branch, Selhurst, Thornton Jn, Tyseley, Westbury, York
3/D	Bescot, Crewe Diesel, Crewe Electric, Cardiff Canton, Motherwell
4/E	Bounds Green, Derby Etches Park, Edinburgh Craigentinny, Eastfield, Eastleigh, Glasgow Shields Rd, Haymarket, Heaton, Immingham, Laira, Old Oak Common, St Phillips Marsh, Stratford, Stewarts Lane, Thornaby, Tinsley, Toton, Vale of Rheidol (Aberystwyth), Willesden
5/F (CEM overhaul)	Bristol Bath Road, Doncaster Works, Neville Hill, Stratford DRS, Springburn Works
6/H (Full rebuild)	RFS Doncaster, Crewe Works, Derby Loco Works, Eastleigh Works, Wolverton Works

THE DIESEL DEPOT | 57

What Depots Do

Class 47 47539 jacked up at Crewe Diesel Depot on February 5, 1994. The depot was a Level 3 facility and will be forever synonymous with the Brush Type 4. (Chris Booth)

Locos at depots on July 14, 1997

Toton		Crewe	
Unscheduled		**Unscheduled**	
31407	Bogies	37424	Compressor
37037	Contaminated Oil	47204	Paint
37097	Lub Oil	47234/302/77/91	Engine repairs
37133/417/667 56108	Low Power	47303	High water temperature
37255	Wheelsets	47627	Valves
37377	Fuel gauges	47747	Braking system
37716	Windows	47759	Axle box
56117	Special tests	47760	Fuel pump
58019	Contaminated coolant	47778	Springs
58033	Engine repairs	47782	Turbo
Scheduled		47785	Test run
37800, 58025/30	Light Overhaul	47799	Special Test
37520/703, 47358/370	Intermediate Overhaul	47976	Break blocks
Accident damage		60079	Loss of Power
60010	Collision damage repairs	**Scheduled**	
37238	Derailment damage	37212, 47767	D-exam

Even at a typical Level 4 depot such as Immingham, the most numerous works were refuelling and A-exams to its own fleet and any visits that had worked to the area on a freight service. A-exams were undertaken as due, and in BR days they could have been at any suitable depot. Scheduled exams, while less frequent and fewer in number, took longer and were planned in advance in order to ensure the required locomotive was worked back to the right depot in time. Immingham's Class 56s, for example, required a B-exam roughly every 300 TOPS (Total Operations Processing System) hours, and as one became imminent the individual loco was pre-assigned ('tagged') on TOPS by Regional Maintenance Control to come to its home depot at a specific time on a nominated day.

To spread the work, B-exam frequency could be flexed a little, with some carried out slightly early, others slightly late. C-exams at 1,200 hours, Ds at 3,600

Buxton Depot could attract all sorts of locos used on stone traffic in the area. It was only a Level 2 facility when 45037 paid a visit on May 18, 1985.
(Rail Photoprints/Brian Robbins)

58 THE DIESEL DEPOT

What Depots Do

Toton's Level 4 status allowed it to perform E-exams as well as major component work. Class 58 58044 *Oxcroft Opencast* is raised up on jacks on Road 15, which had strengthened floors to cope with the weight. (Chris Booth)

and F-exams at 7,200 all took a considerable amount of time and thus required a fair degree of planning to ensure they were adequately spread so not too many locos were stopped at one time and a depot wasn't overwhelmed with work. In the latter days of BR, the 'shopping' of locos (formerly classified repairs) usually meant sending them to a BRML workshop, and this was planned by CRCC (Contract Repair Control Centre) that liaised with the sub-sector managers about the work required. A look at what locos were at Crewe and Toton on July 14, 1997 shows that scheduled maintenance often made up only a small part of a depot's work. More common were the running repairs and faults from which an aging diesel fleet was increasingly suffering.

The famous Barrow Hill Roundhouse in BR days on May 11, 1985. A satellite for Tinsley, it regularly housed several Class 08s from the parent depot for shunting the local yards – as seen here with 08141, 08208, 08172, 08208, 08266 and 08485.
(Rail Photoprints/Gordon Edgar)

Locos at Immingham July 14, 1997

37682	Speedo
37708	Control relay
47476	Coolant leak
47972	Air leak
56006	Defective Battery
56038/98	Low power
56078	Vibrations
56101	Compressor

Sectorisation

Sectorisat

Immaculate Tinsley-based 47146 in Railfreight Distribution colours passes Newport in July 1997. RfD was formed in 1988, but what remained of it was eventually swallowed up by EWS on March 12, 1997. (Rail Photoprints)

60 THE DIESEL DEPOT

Sectorisation

From a regional management structure to a business aligned by sectors, the 1980s heralded major changes for BR and its diesel depots. A key development was Foster Yeoman ordering four locomotives in November 1984. The specification stipulated 95% reliability, something BR acknowledged that neither its existing Class 56, nor other options could provide. Foster Yeoman rebuilt its Merehead Quarry depot in 1985 to provide a well-equipped three-track shed. The depot was the first privately owned and operated main line facility on BR and it exemplified the modern, dedicated method of maintaining locomotives. Come March 31, 1986 BR had 26 depots with a main line diesel or electric allocation, along with another 35 depots that only had diesel shunters on their books.

In 1987, the Roundel Design Group was commissioned by BR to design plaques that were to be fitted to locos to denote their home depot. They were aluminium cast plates and on Thursday October 15, 1987 Ripple Lane Depot held a press day to launch them. Most of the major maintenance depots received a plaque design alongside some staff-based suggestions for smaller depots and, in some cases, wagon works.

Depot symbols as of 1993

Depot	Code	Symbol
Acton		Players Mask
Allerton	AN	Winged 'A' and Wheel
Barry	BY	Galleon
Bristol Barton Hill	BK	Unicorn
Bescot	BS	Saddle
Brush Loughborough	LB	Falcon
Buxton	BX	Millstone
Crewe Diesel	CD	Cheshire Cat
Crewe Electric	CE	Eagle
Cardiff Canton	CF	Goat
Carlisle Currock	KC	Fox
Derby EDU	ZA	Ram
Dollands Moor	DL	Invicta and EU stars
Eastfield	ED	West Highland Terrier
Eastleigh	EH	Spitfire
Exeter	EZ	Pterodactyl
Grangemouth	GM	Viking Ship (only fitted to wagons)
Healey Mills	HM	Woollen Mill
Hither Green	HG	Oast Houses
Immingham	IM	Star
Ipswich WRD	IP	Suffolk Punch horse
Knottingley	KY	Pit Winding-wheel
Laira – Plymouth	LA	Ship (Mayflower)
Leicester	LR	Panther
March	MR	Hare (not accepted)
Margam	MG	Kite
Motherwell	ML	Hammer and Anvil
RfD		Class 92 and Wagon
Ripple Lane	RL	Flame
Saltley	SY	Seagull
Stewarts Lane	SL	Battersea Power Station
Southampton WRD	SZ	Ocean Liner
St Blazey	BZ	Lizard
Stratford	SF	Cockney Sparrow (later revised)
Thornaby	TE	Kingfisher
Tinsley	TI	Yorkshire Rose
Toton	TO	Cooling Towers
Unallocated		Bison
Westbury	WY	White Horse
Willesden	WN	Greyhound (not accepted)

THE DIESEL DEPOT

Sectorisation

Reclassification

In early 1987, BR undertook a rationalisation review of its loco and rolling stock maintenance policy. Under the new scheme depots and works were classified between levels 1 and 6. These levels denoted the capabilities of each depot and are further explained in the 'What depots do' chapter (see pages 56-59). By the summer of 1988 this was down to 17 depots with a main line allocation.

In 1988, Railfreight was split into two divisions: Trainload Freight (TLF) and Railfreight Distribution (RfD). TLF was further split into four subsector companies responsible for aggregates, coal, petroleum, and metals, while RfD took over BR's Freightliner and Speedlink wagon load services. For the 1989/90 financial year, BR published an overhaul programme for its locos that showed where most of the major overhauls were being done at the time. British Rail Maintenance Limited, Doncaster had the bulk of the work, with 137 F-exams spread across Classes 31, 37/5, 47/0, 47/3, 47/4, 56 and 58, along with 12 G-exams to 12 Class 56s. BRML Springburn had 32 F-exams scheduled to Class 37 and 47s, while RFS Industries was allocated a tranche of 08 and 09s for general repairs. Interestingly, Stratford DRS had 9 F-exams on Class 47s, Laira had 16 Class 37/0 G-exams, while Eastleigh had five Class 33 F-exams. BREL Crewe received only Class 08s for general repairs.

In the 1988/9 FY, BR's freight businesses made an overall profit of £69m, despite RfD making losses of £65m. In 1990, TLF and RfD were constituted as separate business sectors as part of the 'Organising for Quality' (OfQ) strategy being pursued by BR. Under OfQ the BR sectors were given greater autonomy and became responsible for asset-ownership and their respective bottom lines.

By the end of the 1980s the decade had seen the loss of 12 diesel classes. Naturally this led to efficiency gains in stores, maintenance and, ultimately, a rationalisation of BR's depots. In 1989, sites disposed of by BREL included Derby Carriage and Wagon Works, York Works, Crewe Works, Derby Loco Works, Doncaster Works and Shildon Works. They were taken over by a Swedish conglomerate, which in 1992 was bought out by ABB to become ABB Transportation.

In 1990, BRML announced that, due to excess capacity, one maintenance facility had to close; Stratford in East London was chosen. Class 31 31165 was the final loco to receive attention at the facility and it was also repainted

Depots with main line and shunting loco allocations on March 31, 1986

Eastern		London Midland		Southern		Western		Scottish	
170	Tinsley	248	Toton	80	Stewarts Lane	156	Cardiff Canton	120	Eastfield
121	Immingham	172	Crewe Diesel	71	Eastleigh	85	Bath Road	95	Haymarket
116	Gateshead	157	Willesden			52	Old Oak Common	45	Inverness
102	Stratford	93	Bescot			49	Laira	30	Motherwell
85	March	37	Crewe Electric			21	Landore	18	Glasgow (Shields)
79	Thornaby	29	Cricklewood						
		58	Kingmoor						
		12	Kingmoor Yard						

Depots with main line and shunting loco allocations on March 31, 1986

Eastern		London Midland		Southern		Western		Scottish	
15	Colchester	22	Allerton	17	Selhurst	6	Margam	7	Thornton
15	York	18	Derby	9	Ashford	4	Gloucester	6	Ayr
12	Doncaster	13	Longsight DD			4	Reading	4	Aberdeen
11	Cambridge	13	Tyseley			3	Swindon	3	Grangemouth
10	Neville Hill	12	Bletchley			2	St Blazey		
10	Norwich	8	Chester			1	Penzance		
9	Hull Botanic Gardens	5	Wigan Springs Branch						
9	Healey Mills	3	Birkenhead North						
6	Bounds Green	2	Leicester						
5	Frodingham								
4	Barrow Hill								
4	Knottingley								
3	Lincoln								
3	Shirebrook								

Main line allocations exclude steam, departmental locos, HSTs, DMUs and EMUs.

Depots with a main line loco allocation in summer 1988

Eastern	London Midland	Southern	Western	Scottish
Immingham	Bescot	Eastleigh	Bristol	Eastfield
Stratford	Crewe Diesel	Stewarts Lane	Cardiff	Haymarket
Thornaby	Toton		Laira	Inverness
Tinsley			Old Oak Common	Motherwell

The variety of BR diesel types, even in 1981, is illustrated by this photo of Doncaster Works on October 4 that year. Visible are 03063, 50008, 50009, 50041, 50016, 37267 and 31223, as well as a further unidentified 03. As the number of types was reduced, so the need for so many workshops diminished, and many were sold off in the early 1990s. (Rail Photoprints/John Chalcraft)

Sectorisation

Once famous depots, such as Haymarket in Edinburgh, saw a significant loss of traffic under sectorisation as freight locos were assigned to other Scottish facilities. Class 55 Deltic 55011 *The Royal Northumberland Fusiliers* starts up at Haymarket on June 4, 1978. Today the depot is a major ScotRail facility, but is home only to a DMU fleet. (Rail Photoprints/John Chalcraft)

into a version of BR green livery complete with small yellow warning panels. Stratford Level 5 Depot closed its doors for the final time on March 31, 1991 after a 77-year career.

Mail and postal services came under the Rail Express Systems' brand in 1991. Bristol Bath Road lost its parcels' sponsored Class 47/4s when they were re-allocated to Crewe Diesel Depot, and this allowed Bath Road to take on more InterCity work. While hoping to attain BS5750 certification, the depot was used to maintain BR Class 47/8 long-range locos for InterCity's Cross Country business. Notably, the depot also had its own paint shop in the track-machine maintenance shed at Marsh Junction and that was where most of Bath Road's Class 47/8s received their InterCity Swallow colours.

Pushing the dedicated locos to dedicated depots and the traffic ideology of sectorisation was the experimental Tinsley-based automotive pool FDAA, which contained 13 Class 47/0s and 47/3s. The idea behind the pool was to provide a dedicated fleet for the main flows of automotive traffic between the West Midlands and Swindon/Oxford, Bathgate and Dover. In an effort to improve reliability, even A-exams were undertaken at the same depot – Saltley.

At the start of the 1990s, apart from RfD, BRs freight sectors were arguably in their best shape for several decades. From this high point, however, the building industry suffered a huge slump, and TL-Construction lost 30% of its tonnage between 1988/9 and 1993/4. The period also saw the closure of Ravenscraig Steelworks in 1992, meaning a loss of 23% in tonnage along with £14m in annual revenue, and with only £4.5m in cost savings for TL-Metals. Worse, however, were the TL-Coal losses, as the sector accounted for 60% of TLF's total turnover. Huge changes in the electricity generation industry were afoot, and generation by gas massively increased, while UK coal production decreased from an average of 129m tonnes per year in the 1970s to 94m tonnes in 1991 and a mere 49m tonnes by 1994. This meant that although imports offset some of the UK losses, the sector still suffered a loss of 38% in tonnage and 37% in real income. Between 1988/9 and 1993/4 TLF turnover went down 35% and volume by 30%, while costs only reduced by 23%. In an effort to balance the books, loco and wagon numbers were slashed, staff numbers were reduced by 2,000 to 12,000, and depot rationalisation had to come.

The bottom line is king

What's noticeable in this period is that, while traffic losses were the key driver for closure in the 1980s, the accountant was the arbiter of a depot's future in the 1990s. The desire to make each business unit fully accountable and, wherever possible, each depot singularly accountable to one business sector, was at the forefront of decision making. A depot's age profile was important, as management considered the cost implications of making large numbers of men redundant. Training men on different traction was usually a five-day course and wasn't seen as a problem, whereas acquiring route knowledge typically took three weeks for an averagely complicated route, and so any depot closures had to be made with a mind to this requirement. The potential cost of light engine movements was also appreciated and depot closures were not to be made where these would substantially increase. One Type 5 loco that was required due to the depot being remote from the traffic cost the rough equivalent of seven drivers over a year.

It was also noted that depots with a strong tradition of a thirst for work and lack of militancy were the more desirable to keep. Finally, in the most interesting and telling point on the pitfalls of fragmentation and ensuing privatisation, TLF noted: "While each area manager sought to shed the costs and responsibilities of depots in their area to improve their own bottom lines, a lack of co-operation and bigger-picture thinking was precluding the best results from being obtained overall." Exemplifying the measures they were looking to take, was the area manager for West Midlands Freight who wrote a letter on traincrew strategy on September 4,

BR extinct classes in the 1980s

Class	Year
01	1981
05	1981
06	1981
13	1985
24	1980
25	1987
27	1987
40	1985
44	1980
45	1989
46	1984
55	1982

Thornaby in the North East retained its importance as a major diesel depot well into the privatised era. Prior to that it was an important facility for Trainload Freight locos. Class 60s 60038 (Metals) and 60030, plus a construction sector example outside, were on shed at Thornaby on June 4, 1993. (Michael Rhodes)

Stratford Level 5 Depot closed its doors for the final time on March 31, 1991 after a 77-year career, and the site is now occupied by Stratford International Station. Class 15 8204, Class 46 156 and Class 47s 1536 and 1640 occupy the servicing shed on October 9, 1907; the workshop building is to the left. (Rail Photoprints/John Medley)

THE DIESEL DEPOT | 63

Sectorisation

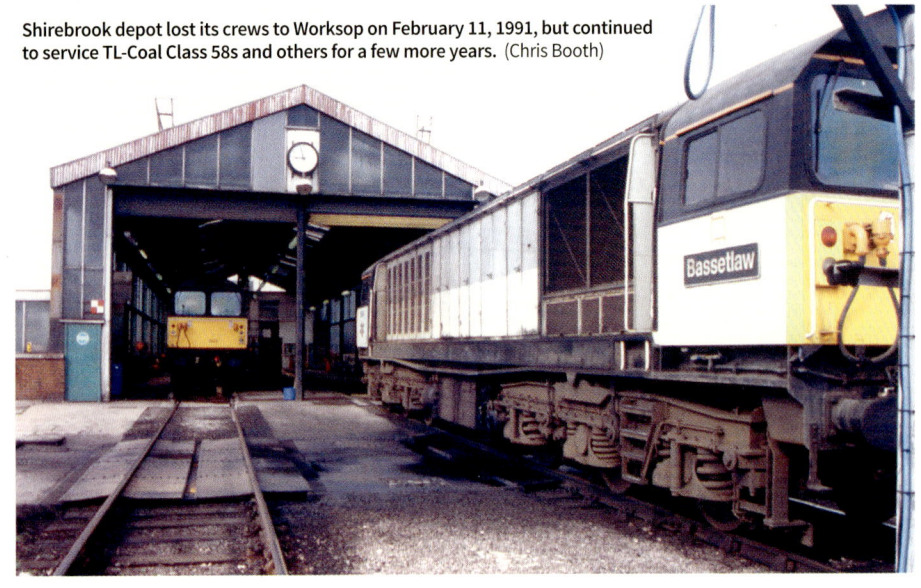

Shirebrook depot lost its crews to Worksop on February 11, 1991, but continued to service TL-Coal Class 58s and others for a few more years. (Chris Booth)

The WR's Bristol Bath Road was once a very important depot with a large loco allocation and workforce. The changing face of the railway saw it gradually lose work as loco use declined, and under sectorisation diesels were moved elsewhere. Three sectors, RES (47476), InterCity (47834) and Network SouthEast (47711) are illustrated in this image taken on June 27, 1991. (Rail Photoprints/John Chalcraft)

1992 in which he proposed the extremely radical and not yet evaluated (never mind validated) proposal to close Stoke-on-Trent, Gloucester and Saltley, with their work transferring to Bescot and Newport, along with the closure of Rugby and the covering of its work by Stonebridge Park and Crewe.

In 1993, TLF undertook a review of its traincrew depots and provisions with a view to streamlining its assets and reducing its associations with other BR sectors, including, where possible, trying to make each depot the responsibility of a single TLF division. In Scotland TLF pulled out of Stranraer on March 22, 1992 and Grangemouth Depot was earmarked for closure in March the following year, with the residual petroleum traffic in Scotland being concentrated upon Motherwell. The end of March 1992 also saw TLF pull out of Fort William, Oban, Inverness, Perth and Queen Street depots, thus leaving an ongoing requirement at Ayr, Millerhill and Motherwell.

In the Tees and Tyne areas of the North East, Thornaby had an ongoing TL-Metals requirement. Meanwhile, dependent upon future coal trends, TL-Coal still needed a presence at Tyne, South Dock and Blyth depots. In the North West area, Warrington and Carnforth were seen as key TLF depots, while Carlisle was to continue as a multisector depot as well as Workington, with a natural wastage of men to reduce its size. Wigan Springs Branch was to see its train crew depot closed and the men moved to Regional Railways (RR) at Wigan Wallgate Station, while Garston, Ellesmere Port and Ditton all had uncertain futures. Crewe was seen as a key RfD depot, but was to lose its TLF work. On South Humberside, Immingham was the only depot with a long-term future

and Frodingham was to become an out-base signing-on point for Immingham in April 1993. In the Yorkshire Freight area, York had been exited and TLF work from Hull had moved to Skipton where TL-Construction had an ongoing requirement. Finally Doncaster, Knottingley and Healey Mills were all to be trimmed to match TL-Coal requirements.

In the West Midlands, Stoke was closed in March 1993, with its work transferred to Crewe and Bescot. The once bustling depot at Saltley was suffering a significant fall in its workload, as RR intended to be out of there by October 1993. With Didcot Power Station only taking imported coal, Didcot and Toton men were slated to take over any remaining TLF work, leaving only RfD with an interest in Saltley, which was seen at the time as having perhaps only 18 months left. RR was to exit Rugby Depot and from October 1993 it was to take over Tyseley Depot.

Finally, in order to exit a number of depots, TLF work was to be moved from Wolverhampton to Bescot and from Shrewsbury to Hereford. In Wales, Hereford, Margam, Barry and Newport had secure futures, but Cardiff Tidal disappeared in April 1993 and TLF was looking to avoid its last few turns at Cardiff Canton. Westbury and Didcot were long-term traincrew depots, while RfD had a continued interest in St Blazey, with limited petroleum work at Plymouth and Exeter. The key freight depot in the Southern Freight area was Hither Green, and TLF was planning a new depot at Acton in order to pull out of Old Oak Common, along with Swindon, Brighton and Gillingham by the end of March 1993. Meanwhile, Eastleigh, Ashford, Dover and

Stonebridge Park all had uncertain futures. In the Anglia region only Ipswich had a long-term future with RfD. March and Peterborough were under review for closure, TL-Construction had got out of King's Cross, and RfD was reviewing its association with Ripple Lane and Parkstone, the latter being dependent upon the future of the Freightliner Terminal.

Looking at the Midlands area in detail, it's clear to see that it experienced some of the most significant changes. The signing-on point at Tibshelf Sidings closed in 1987, and Coalville shut in October 1990, with its 45 train crew either retiring or transferring to other depots. On February 11, 1991, Barrow Hill and Shirebrook Traincrew depots both closed and their 170 drivers moved to Worksop's new £700,000 depot. Locos still received attention at Shirebrook.

In the late 1980s Buxton had serviced DMUs and locos, with its drivers working passenger services one day and perhaps pairs of Class 37s to Washwood Heath the next. TLF and Provincial North-West both wished to retain a presence in Buxton and as a result the train crews were split on May 12, 1994. The passenger men were retained in a room on Buxton's station platform, while a new TLF West signing-on point at Peak Forest was established. At Derby, InterCity Midland Main Line lost its RR, Departmental and TLF work to concentrate solely on InterCity passenger turns. The TL-Coal turns to Denby went to Toton, TL-Metals to Tinsley and the Washwood Heath turns from Peak Forest

Smaller depots, such as Frodingham, waned considerably in the final years of the sectorisation period, with many disappearing after privatisation. This view, taken on July 29, 1992, finds 20104, 20137 and 20165 and an unidentified Class 37 in the servicing shed, while stored to the left are 20076, 20061, 08508, 20043, 20025, 20042. (Michael Rhodes)

64 THE DIESEL DEPOT

www.railwaysillustrated.co.uk

Sectorisation

Buxton was a depot that should have had a more secure future, as TLF and Provincial North-West both wished to retain a presence there in the early 1990s. In the event, freight crews moved to Peak Forest and the depot was progressively run down and finally demolished in March 2016. In October 1985, 20075, 31285 and 45005 share the facility with a resident Class 104 DMU. *(Rail Photoprints)*

were crewed at Derby by Leicester's TL-Construction men. The Crewe and Lincoln passenger services were taken over by Nottingham Eastcroft Depot, which had lost its freight workings to Toton in May 1993 in order to become an exclusively RR depot with just DMU turns. Train crews at Sheffield Station became ever more restricted to local passenger turns and the once mighty yard and depot at Tinsley saw a reduction in men in April 1993 from 88 to 57. Eventually, TL-Steel pulled out, so it became exclusively RfD. Finally, the remaining TLF turns at St Pancras and Bedford were covered by Leicester.

Final carve up

The drive for greater efficiency and responsibility for each business sector's finances meant that in the final years of BR the sectorised freight companies and shadow private firms made some surprising depot openings and elevation in status of others, as they strived to increase their independent capabilities. Wigan Springs Branch had lost its main line allocation in October 1982, with Crewe, and latterly Toton, providing most of its locos. But as RES and Mainline took over Crewe and Toton respectively, Trainsrail concentrated more than 80 locos at Springs Branch and even elevated it to Level 4 status as one of its key facilities.

In 1994, TLF South East opened a new one-track depot in the triangle of lines at Didcot. On July 23, 1995, RES adapted a section of the Wagon Works at Bristol Barton Hill to open a one-track depot, and at the same time vacated Bristol Bath Road. Also evident was the increasing market for loco maintenance, with Loadhaul sending Class 56s to Brush Falcon Works at Loughborough and to ABB Crewe Works for overhaul and repaint. With privatisation imminent, BR's depots had been carved up and distributed amongst the business units, ready for sale.

TLF 1990s Resources

More than 16,400 employees throughout the UK
More than 500 diesel locos
25 loco depots
11 wagon repair depots
51 traincrew depots
975 private sidings and terminals served

TLF Involvement at 71 Depots in 1993

Significant scale Long-term	Small scale Long-term	Medium-term future	Short-term
Ayr	Thornton	Garston	Grangemouth
Millerhill	Motherwell	Saltley	Fort William
Carnforth	Carlisle	Plymouth	Oban
Warrington	Ditton	Swindon	Inverness
Bescot	Chester	March	Perth
Margam/Port Talbot	Llandudno Junction	South Dock	Queen Street
Barry	Crewe	Blyth	Stranraer
Newport	Exeter		Elsmere Port
Hereford	Ashford		Manchester Piccadilly
Westbury	Stratford		Longsight
Didcot	Parkstone		Stoke
Hither Green	Peterborough		Wolverhampton
Leicester	Skipton		Shrewsbury
Toton			Gloucester
Worksop			Cardiff Tidal
Immingham			Cardiff Canton
Doncaster			Old Oak Common
Knottingley			Eastleigh
Healey Mills			Brighton
Thornaby			Gillingham
Tyne			Ripple Lane
			King's Cross
			St Pancras
			Bedford
			Nottingham
			Derby
			Frodingham
			Tinsley
			York
			Hull

THE DIESEL DEPOT | 65

Inverness

Anyone visiting British Rail's most northerly depot at Inverness in the 1960s to 80s found it had a quaint charm and feel that made it well worth the trip. In 1855 the Inverness and Nairn Railway Company built a four-track stone building with a twin gable-style roof. The structure later became the Highland Railway's Lochgorm Works and continued in that capacity until February 1960 when British Railways converted it into a diesel depot. As well as the former works there was a two-track corrugated sheeting building and a single-track facility for underframe washing. The site had used the code 32A, but from January 1, 1949 it became 60A.

Early diesels

The first diesels to arrive at Inverness Depot were Barclay shunters and a single Brush A1A-A1A Type 2. Class 06 D2410 arrived in June 1958 and several more examples soon followed in the shape of D2411, D2412 and D2413 in July, September and October respectively. The first main line locomotive allocated was, surprisingly, Brush Type 2 D5511 in June 1958. While on test the loco made it over the West Highland and Oban lines, along with working main line freights to Carlisle and coal trains between Crew Junction and the Glasgow area. It later underwent tests on the Edinburgh suburban lines with trains of 30 and 35 loaded minfits between South Leith and Gorgie on July 17/18. It later ran between Crew Junction and Carmyle, but with similar loads, and subsequently worked on the Waverley route with both goods and passenger trains.

The second main line loco was BRCW D5303, which had a very brief association with the depot when it was loaned from October to November 1958. On July 27, 1959 Inverness had 32 steam engines on shed, along with three 0-4-0s: D2411 D2423 and D2413. January, February and March 1960 saw English Electric Type 1s D8032/3/4 (20032/3/4) allocated from new, and the same month saw D3553 come and go. From April to September 1960 the depot received 19 BR/Sulzer Type 2s, which made it the first in Scotland to receive what later became Class 24s. They were built at Derby Works and the batch allocated to Inverness was D5114 to D5132. They were the first of the class to be built with the new roof-mounted head code box instead of indicator discs. The locos also featured a recess on the driver's cab side for tablet catcher equipment, which was added in October 1960 at St Rollox Works, Glasgow. Shortly after the delivery of the last of the class, D5117 was transferred to Eastfield (65A) in November 1960 for trials on Glasgow to Edinburgh services. To compensate for the loss, D5326 (26026) came to Inverness from Eastfield, while D5329 (26029) and D5336 (26039) both came from Haymarket. D5116 (24116) also left the depot in December when it was transferred to Polmadie (66A).

1960s developments

After forays to Eastfield and Leith Central Depot, D5116 (24116) and D5117 (24117) returned to Inverness in June 1961. With its diesel numbers growing and expanding its sphere of operation, the sub-sheds at Kyle of Lochalsh, Wick and Helmsdale were run down, the latter two closing on July 31, 1962 and August 31, 1964 respectively. By September 1961 Inverness to Aberdeen services were dominated by diesels and steam was almost entirely absent from the West Highland lines as the BCRW Type 2s proliferated. In addition to the Lochgorm Works buildings, Inverness also had a

Inverness

roundhouse engine shed, and diesels were no strangers to its turntable. What were to become Class 06, 20, 24, 26, and even North British Type 2s (Class 21/29), were all pictured around the turntable. With steam on its way towards eradication, Perth's resignalling in March 1962 saw the number of through trains from Inverness to Glasgow and Edinburgh increase. In May 1962 steam-hauled passenger trains from Edinburgh Waverley finished, and Inverness Depot closed to steam on June 30, 1962.

The Derby-built BR/Sulzer Type 2s (Class 24) received small yellow warning panels at Inverness and, in general, the locos were overhauled at the former Great North of Scotland Railway (GNSR) Inverurie workshop until it closed and work was transferred to Glasgow's St Rollox Works. There was an announcement in January 1965 that Inverness' Type 2s would receive twin sealed-beam headlights for use in the far north.

Inverness' diesels travelled over a wide area and D5119 (24119) was noted on the first day of the dieselised 2025 Perth to Carlisle parcels service on March 2, 1966; it also worked the 0610 Carlisle to Perth parcels the following day. For at least a week in 1967 D5116 was away from Inverness to help coal trains in the Ayr region, but 1968 saw it working on a local service on the Waverley route shortly before it closed.

The 1970s, TOPS and loco swaps

In 1970 Inverness' locos covered a wide array of services, with perhaps the most appealing being the passenger trains to Kyle of Lochalsh, Wick and Thurso. Interestingly, three locos would out-stable overnight, two at Wick and one at Thurso. They worked the first passenger trains of the day from Wick and Thurso and a goods train from Wick.

Several Barclay 0-4-0s had worked at Inverness harbour

ABOVE: A typical 1980s scene at Inverness, with 27049, 47617, 37261 and 47614 standing between duties on April 19, 1986. (Gavin Morrison)

BELOW: Inverness depot on September 4, 1979 with, from left to right, 25240, 26014, 26025, 26036, 20080, 20102 and 40151. The pair of 20s had arrived from Grangemouth with bitumen for the siding at Culloden and parked their train in Inverness yard; it was later tripped out to Culloden by a Class 25. (Michael Rhodes)

THE DIESEL DEPOT | 67

Inverness

Class Allocations

Class	Time Period
06	June 1958-June 1971
08	March 1960, October 1961-98
20	January 1960-October 1966, June 1968-October 1968, June 1979-February 1980
21	May 1960-June 1960
24	April 1960-November 1975
25	November 1975-May 1976, June 1976-June 1979
26	October 1958-November 1958, May 1960-October 1993
27	February 1980-May 1986
31	June 1958-June 1958, July 1958-August 1958
37	October 1981-November 1981, April 1982-March 1994
47	May 1980-January 1993

ABOVE LEFT: Resident Class 26 26014 and visiting 47427 receive attention in the depot's maintenance bays on September 13, 1979. (Michael Rhodes)

LEFT: Inverness' sole Class 06 at the time, D2423, at the depot on September 15, 1970. (Rail Photoprints/ John Chalcraft)

BELOW LEFT: ETH-equipped Class 37/4 were based at Inverness from the mid-1980s, primarily for work on far north services. One of them, 37414, undergoes repairs inside the former Cairngorm Works on April 19, 1986. (Gavin Morrison)

Sample Allocations

September 31, 1960
Class 06	2410/1/2/3/23
Class 20	8032/3/4
Class 24	5114-5132
Class 26	5320-25/28/30/1/3/4/5/7/8/9/40/1/2/3/5/6

September 30, 1965
Class 06	2413/22/23/24
Class 08	3735, 3896, 4095/96
Class 20	8032/33
Class 24	5114-5132
Class 26	5318 5320-5346

December 31, 1970
Class 06	2423
Class 08	3551/55, 3660, 3735, 3896
Class 24	5114-5121/23-5132
Class 26	5330-5346

December 31, 1975
Class 08	08568/620/728/855
Class 25	25030/1/92/3/6
Class 26	26008-46

December 31, 1978
Class 08	08568/620/728/738
Class 25	25062/66/68
Class 26	26013/14/15/18/19/21-46
Class 47	47464/465/469/472/546/550

December 31, 1980
Class 08	08568/620/728
Class 26	26014/15/22-46
Class 27	27003/5/7/8/21/52/108/9/10

Inside the old Cairngorm Works building on March 25, 1981 with 26043, 27001 and 26015 in for repairs. (Michael Rhodes)

since their allocation to Inverness, but from June 1967, D2423 (06006) had soldiered on as the depot's sole example. Its use came to an end in May 1971 when the job was taken over by a Class 08 and D2423 was transferred to Aberdeen (61B). Also during the year, perhaps due to the cramped nature of the shed and confined stabling area, a shunting accident saw English Electric Type 3 6855 (37155) and BR/Sulzer Type 2 5131 collide. While 6855 did suffer significant damage, 5131 came off worse and was later withdrawn. When 5113 (24113) came to Inverness from Eastfield in April 1972, it was notable for being the last of the class built with discs and the first to be based at the depot. One of the initial 19 BR/Sulzer Type 2s to come to Inverness in 1960, 5114, was withdrawn in October 1972 having spent its entire working life at the depot. It was noted at Glasgow Works in 1974 for stripping, removal of its cabs and eventual scrapping.

On May 6, 1973 the depot received the TOPS code IS. For a very brief period in December that year Class 47 1635 (47053) came from Tinsley before being swapped with 47516 from Haymarket in order to give Inverness a Class 47 for driver training. While there, it often worked a Milburn to Millerhill service as far as Perth before returning on a northbound parcels. In June 1974 it was reallocated to Haymarket and during the year the Highland line saw an increased use of Type 4s. Meanwhile, 5112 (24112) and 5113 (24113) bolstered the Class 24 allocation at Inverness with their arrival in February 1974, followed by 24102, 24103 and 24104 from Eastfield in the May. As the year ended 24111 was added to the IS allocation, but was returned to Eastfield depot in March 1975. The last inward transfer of a Class 24 to Inverness was 24110 in May 1975. By that time, although none were ever based at Inverness, Class 40s had become quite common on the Glasgow and Edinburgh to Inverness services. With the increased number of Type 4s working the Highland main line, more and more Type 2s were finding themselves relegated to freight turns.

In the 1970s pairs of Class 20s were working to Invergordon with block trains of alumina wagons for the smelter, along with pairs of Class 24s and 26s on pipe traffic from Invergordon to Maud (on the Fraserburgh branch). Classes 24 and 26 worked passenger and freight trains while Class 40s and occasional Class 47s were worked to Invergordon on general freight, including air-braked services and bulk grain trains from Doncaster to Muir of Ord. Other freight serviced the BP oil siding at Lairg, the distilleries at Strathmill, Kennethmont and Chivas, as well as the goods yards at Inverness, Nairn, Forres, Elgin East and Huntly, where timber was loaded.

BR's Class 24 fleet was being run down in the mid-1970s with storage and withdrawals gathering pace. All of Eastfield's examples were stored in August 1975 and an inroad to the Inverness fleet was made with 24104 in the same month. In September 24121/3/5/6/8 were all transferred to Haymarket, along with 24113/5/6/8 the following month, during which time 24102/3 and 24132 were put in store. With the transfer of 24117/9/24/7/9/30 to Haymarket and 24125 going into store, Inverness had lost its Class 24 allocation for good. Except for 24116 and 24117, these transfers had been the first for the group of 19 that came to Inverness in 1960. As they left Inverness, the Class 24s had their sealed beam headlights removed for use on a number of Class 26s. September to November 1975 saw an influx of Class 26s mainly from Haymarket, these being 26008-15, 26017-26 and 26028.

Although the Class 24s were now based at Haymarket, they still had regular turns over the Highland main line to Inverness until at least October 1976. When Inverness' last Class 24s left the depot in October and November 1975, it simultaneously received its first Class 25s – 25030, 25031, 25092, 25093 and 25096. In May 1976 the Class 25s were all re-allocated back to Eastfield and this briefly left Inverness with only Class 08s and 26s on its books. It wasn't devoid of Class 25s for long, with 25062, 25064, 25083 being received in June 1976; 25092 and 25093 also made a brief return in July, but were transferred to Eastfield within the month. The start of the winter 1976 timetable brought the use of the last few ex-Inverness Class 24s to an end; they were laid up by October and withdrawn in the December. This left only Crewe to persevere with the last of the class.

Class 25s 25068/226/8/9/231/3/4/8 all came to

The depot layout in September 1968. (Alex Fisher)

Apart from two spells at Eastfield, 47550 was an Inverness loco from May 1978 until March 1989. It stands outside the depot on September 24, 1988. (Gavin Morrison)

THE DIESEL DEPOT | 69

Inverness

Inverness ready for the start of the summer timetable in May 1977. Their stay was brief, for the following May timetable change saw them all, except for 25068, transferred to Eastfield. Another transfer was 25083, which left only 25062/4/8 at IS. Replacing the Class 25s were six ETH-equipped Class 47s – 47464/5/9/72/546/50. During June 1979 the depot's last three Class 25s, 25062/6/8, were reallocated to Eastfield and coming the other way were three Class 20s, 20007/20/85. However, Class 25s continued to visit for several more years.

In the summer of 1979 Inverness had three booked shunting duties and these were for an air-braked pilot engine at the station, one at Inverness Milburn Yard and another for yard and local trips to Inverness Harbour, the coal depot and Millburn Yard, as required. The three Class 20s left in February 1980, but arriving were the first examples of the Class 27 with 27108/9/10. Their numbers quickly swelled and a total of 32 examples called Inverness their home at various times until May 1986 when 27025/26/42/48/49/50/64/65 were transferred away.

The 1980s and slow rundown

In May 1980, 47424 came from Haymarket to replace 47465, which was sent to Toton. However, in August 47424 left for Eastfield in a swap with 47467. In 1981 Inverness still had three shunting diagrams covering the station pilot, Milburn Yard and Inverness Goods Yard/Harbour/station motor rail pilot respectively.

In October and November 37014 had a brief spell allocated to the depot, it being a precursor to the influx of Class 37s that came later. Another four Class 37s arrived in 1982 and several more joined them, along with additional Class 47s throughout the 1980s. Few of either the Class 37s or 47s spent more than a year at the depot. By February 1983, Inverness' Class 08 diagrams had been reduced to two. One covered the station, while the other serviced Milburn Yard and made trips as required to the harbour. In August 1983, goods trains to Kyle of Lochalsh ceased and so too would the attractive sight of a mixed goods and passenger train on the line. In May 1985 Inverness still had two Class 08 diagrams, one for a dual-braked loco to shunt Inverness Station and Motorail siding along with the carriage sidings. The second dual-braked 08 shunted Milburn Yard and made trips to the wagon repair shops. In May 1987, the two 08 diagrams required a dual-braked locomotive for the station/Motorail pilot and an air-braked one for Milburn Yard and the wagon works trips.

Following the River Ness viaduct collapse on February 7, 1989 ScotRail moved to establish a temporary traction and rolling stock maintenance depot at Muir of Ord. The single track depot serviced the isolated locos, coaches and DMUs for more than a year until the bridge was rebuilt. With the use of loco-hauled trains in the Highlands coming to end, by late 1990 Inverness had received 12 two-car Class 156s DMUs. Locos still featured quite strongly though, and interestingly every single Class 26 spent at least some time based at Inverness at one point in its life. It even managed to have 58 different Class 47s allocated between May 1978 and January 1993 when the last example, 47643, was transferred.

The use of Class 26s came to an end in October 1993 when its last remaining examples were withdrawn. This also meant that in late 1993 Motherwell resumed its place as the Scottish depot with the largest loco allocation (43 compared with 41 at Inverness). At this time the Inverness inventory consisted mainly of Class 37s and incredibly it had 102 different examples allocated to it between October 1981 and March 1994 when it lost its last 27 as part of the pre-privatisation re-organisation of BR's loco fleets. Marking the end of main line locos at Inverness was the naming of 37025 *Inverness TMD* in March 1994, it being specially repainted into BR Large Logo livery from Civil Engineers Dutch livery.

BELOW LEFT: On a damp morning at Inverness, BR/Sulzer Type 2 5121 and BRCW Type 2 5336 wait to leave with trains for Wick and Kyle of Lochalsh respectively on September 15, 1970. Soon to be a Class 24, 5121 was originally allocated to the depot in 1960. (Rail Photoprints/John Chalcraft)

BELOW RIGHT: Following withdrawal, the three ETHEL Class 25s stand in the yard near the depot on March 22, 1992. (Gavin Morrison)

Oddities

An interesting development involving Inverness was the conversion of the former Class 25 locomotives into ETHELs (Electric Train Heating Ex-Locomotives). Their initial use was on the Fort William Sleeper services, but after Class 37s with ETH were introduced they were used on steam specials. They had all been placed into store at Inverness by 1992. 97251 (formerly 25305) was even allocated to Inverness between September 1992 and March 1993. The three ETHELs were sent to MC Metals Glasgow in August 1994 for breaking up.

Like most large depots, the Inverness Class 08 contingent saw a profusion of different examples over the years but, throughout, a notable Inverness stalwart was 08754. It was new to Corkerhill in January 1961, had a brief spell at Leith Central from 1968 to 1969 and then was transferred to Polmadie until 1972. It then went to Eastfield until November 1981, when it came to Inverness. Barring a brief transfer away between July and September 1982, it was still there in 1998, 17 years later. The BR Blue loco even sported a painted white Highland stag on one of its bodyside boxes. The only other Class 08 on the depot's books at the time was 08762, which had been there since October 1991. In 1995, Inverness had a duty for only one Class 08 to cover Milburn Sorting Sidings, trips to the wagon repair shops and shunting at the station. It also had a spare turn for a locomotive to cover the same diagram. The two diagrams were covered by 08 in the ScotRail HASS shunter pool, which variously included 08308/754/762 and 788.

When ScotRail announced that it would cease using loco-hauled trains by the end of 1995, speculation was rife that Inverness would be run down. The depot survived this closure scare in February 1995 when ScotRail confirmed its newly acquired sleeper vehicle fleet would all be based there. At the time the depot had a workforce of 111 and they maintained ScotRail's Sprinter stock as well as undertaking contract work for the InterCity West Coast Train Operating Unit, Transrail and Railtrack's snow clearance train. The 2000s were fairly uneventful for the depot, it continued to use a Class 08, and in July 2012 it was 08308. 08788 came and went, as did other Class 08s, and in 2016, 08523 was resident.

Recent activities

The depot is currently run by Abellio ScotRail and it still uses the 1855 stone building, known today as the Wagon Shop. Next to it is the two-road corrugated-clad building known as the TMD and the single road washout facility that completes the covered roads. Outside is 'Stores Road', which is where any units can be loaded on to a lorry. The old tank road beside it is not normally used, although it has been known to have the 08 stored on it. On the other side of Rose Street is the two-track carriage siding maintenance depot, which BR built in the 1980s. There's a short line known as the 'Cripple Road', and the other is known as the Long Road and can hold six coaches under cover. There are an additional three storage sidings known as 6, 7 and 8 roads along with a 25m-long fuel shed with de-tanking facilities adjacent to Rose Street, which can take a single coach.

In 2016, there were 49 drivers and 39 conductors based at the depot, while on the station there were approximately 15 support staff. The maintenance depot is still going strong and it has approximately 60 staff, including cleaners. The main work today is servicing Class 158 and 170 units; 158701-725 are allocated to Inverness and are undergoing refurbishment to the 'scenic train' standard, which involves the removal of First Class, fitting new power sockets and new seating. Inverness also fuels and undertakes basic repairs to any visiting Class 170s, although 170393-396 and 170470-478 are slightly rarer. Finally, with the sleeper stock based there, Inverness had been undertaking a C3 exam on one sleeper coach at a time.

ABOVE: An elevated view of the depot on April 19, 1986 with 26026, 37261 and 47614 visible; to the right is a pair of Class 37s in the fuel offloading siding. (Gavin Morrison)

BELOW RIGHT: A pair of ScotRail Inverness-based Class 47/4s under repair at the depot on July 8, 1989. To the right is 47461; it was repainted from InterCity livery to the blue stripe variant – the only example to wear this scheme. (Gavin Morrison)

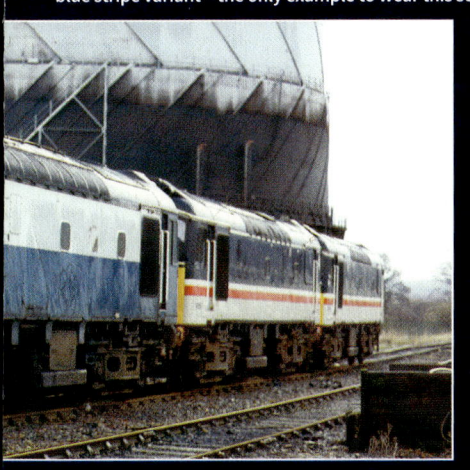

Penzance

Almost at the tip of the South West coastline lies the small Long Rock servicing depot. Today it sees mainly HSTs, the Night Riviera and the occasional charter train, but previously there was a steam shed on the site that, in the Indian summer of the BR Holiday train before its demolition, was a most interesting place that welcomed a range of visiting engines.

Early days

Building a railway line to the extremity of the South West wasn't an easy undertaking due to the gradients and the number of viaducts required. In 1839 a narrow gauge line for mining traffic was opened and this route was later adopted for a broad gauge single line. The first broad gauge Paddington to Penzance service ran in March 1867. From 1875 Penzance had the shed code 153 and as services to the West Country increased and the number of locomotives visiting outgrew its facilities, by 1914 a new engine shed had been built. The main shed had two twin-gable buildings covering two tracks each and was 210ft long by 66ft wide. To the side stood the Lifting Shop, which covered one track and was 84ft by 40ft.

RIGHT: Warship D820 *Grenville* awaits servicing at Penzance after arriving with the down Cornish Rivera in 1962. (Rail-Online)

BELOW: A pair of Class 52s, 1012 *Western Firebrand* and 1046 *Western Marquis* outside the old Penzance Depot steam shed on March 9, 1975. (Roger Geach)

The Boiler House was 30ft by 22ft and there was a 125ft by 15ft office building down the rear side of the shed. The Coal Stage was 32ft by 30ft and had a 45,000-gallon water tank above it. The shed also had a turntable large enough to fit the various sizes of steam engines that ran on the route. In 1947 the depot was home to three Counties, one Castle, six Halls, four Granges, two Moguls, six 4500s and three Pannier Tanks.

From 1950 Newton Abbot was 83A, and under this numbering system the five-road shed at Penzance was designated 83G, with a sub-shed at Helston, St Ives.

Penzance

THE DIESEL DEPOT | 73

Penzance

ABOVE: Class 52 D1040 *Western Queen* inside the depot waiting for either servicing or attention on December 15, 1974. Note the pile of new brake blocks to the right. (Roger Geach)

BELOW: Changing times on the WR in July 1974 as a Western and a Class 50 stand outside the Long Rock shed on a wet summer's day. (Rail Photoprints)

Penzance saw its first diesel allocation in the shape of Class 08 D3514 in August 1958, with D3596/7 following in the September. D3514 had been built in Derby Works and had made the long journey to Laira where it was allocated as new on May 16, 1958 before arriving at Penzance three months later. D3596 and D3597 were both built at Horwich Works and are listed as being new to Penzance in the September, yet both were re-allocated in October – D3596 to Cardiff East Dock and D3597 to Old Oak Common. So did they ever make it all the way to Penzance? The depot never had a main line diesel loco allocation, but over a 30-year period, from August 1958 to October 1988, it had 18 different Class 08s allocated to it and has since seen various other 08s, all drawn from Plymouth Laira's allocation.

Diesel injection

In September 1958 Laira received Warship D800 *Sir Brian Robertson* and in October 1958 it became the first locomotive to take up the class's new diagram on the up 'Cornish Riviera Express' from Penzance to Paddington, no doubt making it one of the first main line diesels to visit the shed at Penzance. In May 1958 Laira had received D600 *Active*, followed by D601 *Ark Royal* in the June. The latter was notable on June 16, 1958 for being the first diesel loco to run non-stop from Paddington to Plymouth, again with the 'Cornish Riviera Express'. From January 1959, the class started to work through to Penzance, making it another diesel type to be seen at the depot. Baby Warships (later Class 22) D6300 and D6301 came to Laira in February 1959 and when the Westerns (later Class 52) also arrived at the Plymouth shed in December 1961, both classes were soon seen at Penzance.

Throughout the 1950s Penzance steam depot had a varied allocation, ranging from 4-6-0 Granges and Countys to 0-6-0PT tank engines. Its steam residents were run down quite quickly in the early 1960s as the influx of visiting diesels from Laira expedited the demise of steam in the West Country. In April 1962, brand new shunter D4161 joined D3514 to double the depot's tally.

After a few withdrawals and many transfers, Penzance was left with just five steam engines that were all re-allocated on October 6, 1962 after it had officially closed to steam that September. From September 1963 the depot was recoded as 84D, but by that time the large diesel facility at Plymouth had opened (designated

Gently ticking over before its next duty 1049 *Western Monarch* shares the depot with a Peak, an 08 shunter and two DMUs on March 9, 1975. (Roger Geach)

Penzance

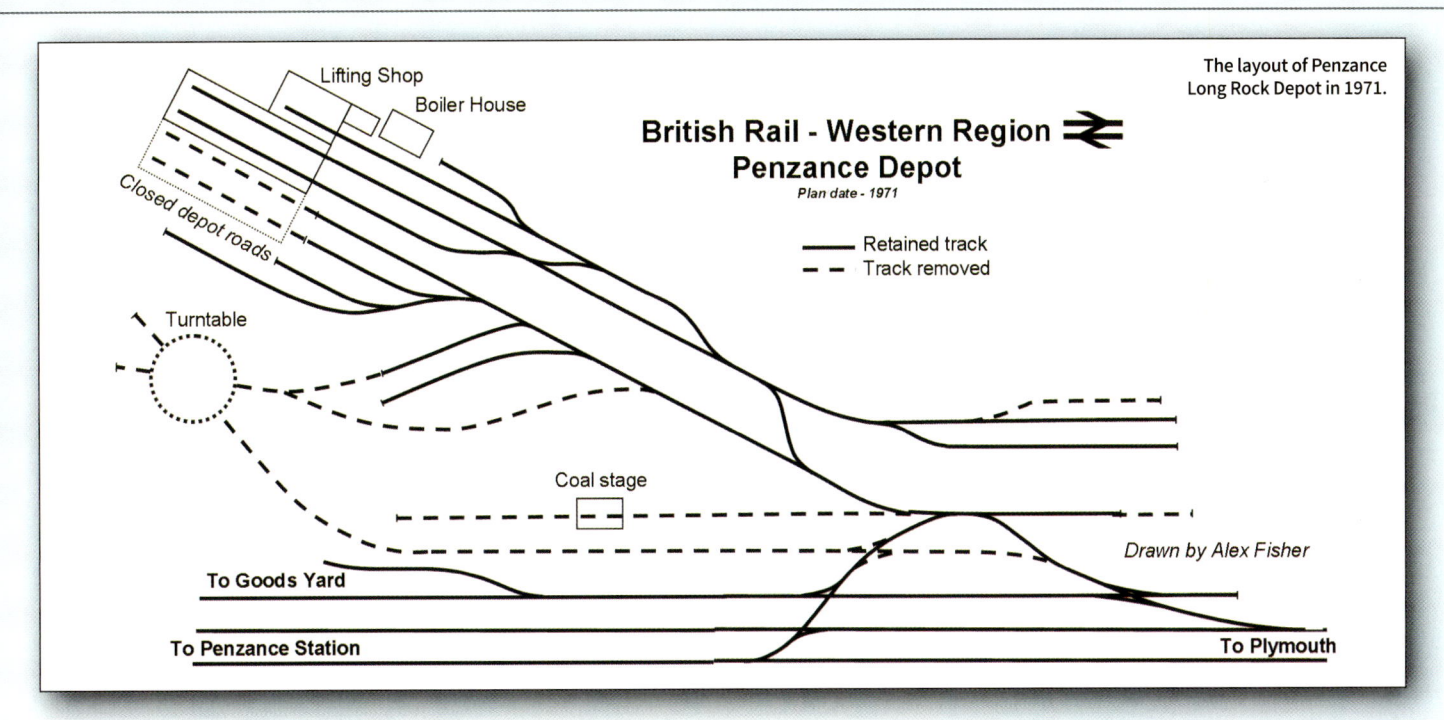

British Rail - Western Region
Penzance Depot
Plan date - 1971

The layout of Penzance Long Rock Depot in 1971.

— Retained track
-- Track removed

Lifting Shop · Boiler House · Closed depot roads · Turntable · Coal stage · To Goods Yard · To Penzance Station · To Plymouth

Drawn by Alex Fisher

84A) which meant that top shed status had passed from Newton Abbot to Plymouth Laira. The very last steam engine to visit Long Rock was Bulleid Pacific 34002 *Salisbury* on May 3, 1964. It was allocated to Exmouth Junction at the time and was eventually preserved and even re-registered for main line use. With steam then a fading memory in the West Country, the turntable was removed in 1966.

After ten years at Long Rock D3514 was re-allocated to Derby in June 1968, but within two weeks it was moved again, this time to Toton and then the LMR division. D4013 was transferred to Penzance from nearby St Blazey to replace D3514. Rationalisation of the depot came in 1968 when two of the four shed roads were removed. Laira and Newton Abbott train crews began learning BR/Sulzer Type 4s (later Class 46s) at the beginning of the 1969 winter timetable in order to allow them to work through to Plymouth and Paignton, rather than undertake a loco change at Bristol. By December 1969, the Class 46s were going all the way to Penzance and, as a result, were to be seen on shed.

With the 'Cornish Riviera Express' still booked for two D800s until the May timetable change in 1970, the diesel depot at Penzance was at its most interesting. In January 1971, D4181 came from Ebbw Junction as a replacement for D4013, which initially went to Bristol Bath Road and then Ebbw Junction. A visit to Long Rock on April 3, 1971 found Penzance-based shunters 4161 and 4181 on shed alongside Laira's Warships 821 and 822 plus Westerns 1005 and 1039, in addition to visiting locos. By the end of the summer 1971 timetable, the Western Region hydraulic fleet was being concentrated at Laira and numbers were dwindling.

The 1970s saw the Penzance depot buildings deteriorate and an air of general decay pervade. A visit in 1972 would have revealed Western Region Class 46s, 47s, 50s and 52s as regular attendees, along with visiting Class 25s and 45s, plus occasional Class 47s from such far flung places as Knottingley and the LMR's Stoke and Birmingham Divisions, on the numerous summer Saturday services. With the first Class 50s coming to Laira in March 1974, the type soon made an appearance at the depot and on March 12, 1974 50027 made its maiden visit, where it was noted alongside D1053 *Western Patriarch*, D1068 *Western Reliance* and Class 47 1665. Also in May 1974, D4181 departed and was transferred to Bristol Bath Road, its place being taken by 08954 from Laira. At this time the depot also welcomed DMUs and the Park Royal viaduct inspection unit operated by Liftec.

At the nearby station, parcels and postal services were very prominent at the time, with trains such as the 4M05 Penzance to Crewe vans and the many services to the North East and Paddington. In June 1974, Long Rock signal box adjacent to the depot was closed. Then, in December, 08840 arrived from St Blazey in a swap for 08928. 08954 left Penzance in April 1976 when it was exchanged with Laira's 08643.

New facilities

With falling glass and a forlorn look about the place, the old steam shed

By the mid-1970s the hydraulics were relinquishing their domination on West of England duties and more diesel electrics were reaching Penzance. Accompanying D1054 *Western Governor* on August 10, 1975 are 45028, 47088 and 47119. (Roger Geach)

THE DIESEL DEPOT 75

Penzance

ABOVE: Typifying the ground conditions at many depots in the 1970s, D1001 *Western Pathfinder* takes a break at Long Rock in 1973. (Rail-Online)

BELOW: Using former steam facilities was never the ideal solution for diesel traction, even after the last steam locos were retired. Entering the shed for servicing is D1057 *Western Chieftain* on October 20, 1974. (Roger Geach)

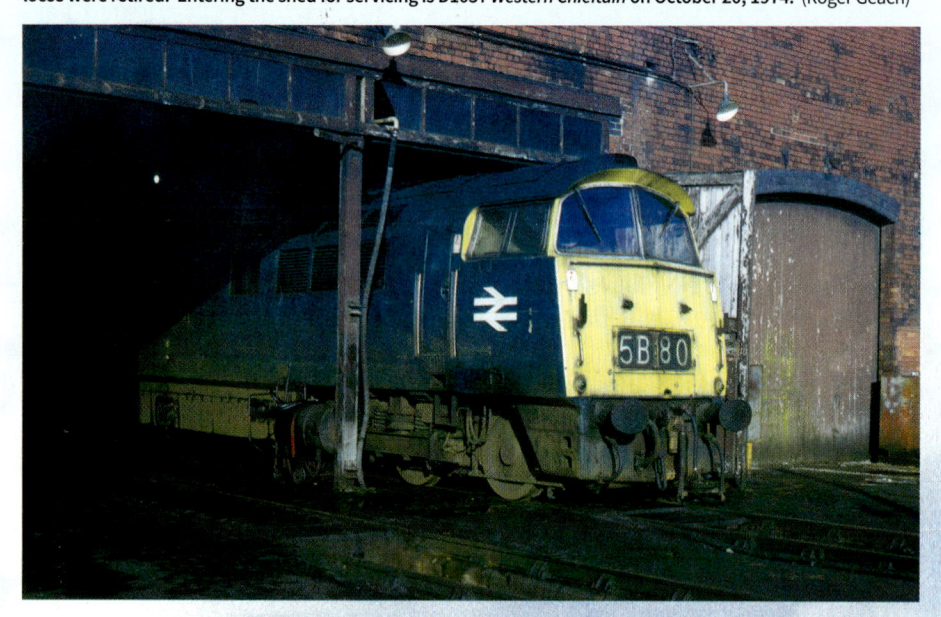

was abandoned in June 1976, even though the new HST depot was still only a steel frame in the October. By the end of the following year the steam shed had been taken down. The new HST depot is situated alongside the main line, which now runs as a single track on the southern side and terminates at Penzance Station, half a mile to the west. The primary building is a 750ft long maintenance shed that can accommodate a full length HST, and there are two lean-to buildings under which HST power cars can be fuelled and serviced simultaneously. There are six long sidings on which HSTs and Voyagers can be stabled, and four smaller sidings for the DMUs that work in the area, along with a small carriage washer and overhead gantry lighting. Train sets may also stable at Laira and work down empty stock if there is no room at Penzance. The depot used to receive its fuel by train, but latterly the fuel storage tanks behind the maintenance shed have been replenished on a daily basis by road deliveries. In total, the new depot cost £1.5m to build and was ready for use in October 1977.

Glory days

Class 08 08840 was re-allocated away from Penzance in July 1978 and 08895 was brought as a replacement. Soon after, 08643 also left, to be replaced by 08941, but this didn't last long as it was usurped by 08641 in August 1979, at a time when the depot had a requirement for two dual-braked Class 08 shunters. One would act as station pilot, with additional responsibility for shunting of the carriage and parcels sidings. The second provided continuous shunting cover for Ponsandane Goods Depot, which received oil tanks. On a Saturday it would also act as a second station pilot and was known to make occasional weekday trips to Hayle Harbour in lieu of the more normal Class 25.

In March 1980, 08895 left Penzance for Laira, which sent 08644 as a replacement. In 1981 it was noted that Penzance still had a requirement for two dual-braked Class 08s. Their duties were the same as they had been in 1979, but they were also used for occasional trips to St Erth and Hayle Harbour. Furthermore, St Blazey Depot at Par kept a spare dual-brake Class 08 as cover for Penzance's own locomotives.

Throughout the 1980s the new facilities continued to see passing locomotive-hauled trains with Class 45s and 46s on a diverse range of passenger services originating from the likes of Wolverhampton, Bristol, Newcastle,

First Great Western Class 47/8 47811 at the Long Rock HST Depot with a Motorail van on January 23, 2000. The HST depot buildings opened in 1977 and remain in use as such today and are also used by CrossCountry Voyagers and the Night Riviera sleeper stock. (Roger Geach)

Penzance

Liverpool, Leeds and York. HSTs, along with Class 50s, were the most common, though; the former on cross-country duties along with the latter to Paddington. Class 47s on the North East-South West cross-country passenger jobs and Class 45s and 47s on the numerous postal and parcel services were also evident. 08641 left for Laira in January 1982 and was replaced by 08949, although that didn't stay long, also leaving for Laira in May 1982 and being exchanged for 08576 until that left Penzance in the August.

From August 1982, 08644 was the last and only loco allocated to Penzance. Its duties encompassed station pilot and shunting Motorail flats, the HST depot, carriage sidings and Ponsandane Goods Depot. The shunter's role remained the same until at least May 1987, and in July 1988 St Blazey's 08801 was noted at Penzance after a collision with a DMU. The depot's sole resident Class 08 (08644) was transferred to Laira in October 1988 and from then on Penzance had no loco allocation.

A Class 08 continued to be used at Penzance, however. 08801 was re-allocated from St Blazey to Laira in October 1988, but the BR blue shunter continued to cover the Penzance shunting diagram. In June 1990 it was damaged in another collision, this time with 47538 as it travelled from Long Rock to Penzance Station. Although 47538 sustained only superficial damage it was enough for the large logo blue loco to be put in store, never to see revenue-earning traffic again. The 08 was repaired and soon returned to work at Penzance.

In August 1990, 08644 was stabled at Long Rock in BR general grey livery, but by 1992 the Laira machine had received the name *Ponsandane* and a coat of InterCity livery. In June 1997, Laira's 08641 was noted acting as station pilot at a time when postal services were still common. However, in 2004 the Post Office services ceased, though at the time Penzance still had the 1C01 1930 Penzance to Bristol and the 1C02 0058 Bristol to Penzance services, both including Travelling Post Office vehicles. Despite the loss of postal work the depot was still used by the Class 47s and later 57s that powered the sleepers between Penzance and Paddington.

Quieter days

Moving on to the 2010s, in 2011 the Long Rock pilot loco was due for heavy repairs, so sometime between May 10 and 13 08644 was sent from Laira to Penzance by road. In early January the next year, 08644 suffered a broken crank arm and was taken out of service, its duties being covered by a Class 57. Spare parts to effect repairs were to arrive by road, but when this couldn't be achieved at Long Rock the shunter was propelled onto a low loader by 57603 and taken away to Loughborough's Brush Works on February 15. It returned to Laira on May 25.

In the meantime, 08410 covered Penzance, but when it suffered defects, 08644 was sent from Laira on April 18, 2013 to assume its shunting duties. With the defects repaired, 08410 returned, and 08644 was sent back to Laira August 2. In need of an exam, 08410 left Long Rock on September 30, 2013 by low loader and returned on March 17, 2014. It was in need of attention again in the August, and while it was away 08641 covered the Penzance diagram until November 10, 2015 when 08410 returned once again.

Although today's services aren't as varied and the motive power is certainly less interesting, the depot still sees HSTs and Voyagers stabled overnight. The current workload is five HSTs, two XC Voyagers and three DMUs. There are still long-distance services to Cardiff Central, Paddington, Manchester Piccadilly and Glasgow Central. The epic 0820 SX 1V60 from Aberdeen to Penzance also runs and completes its 773-mile journey to the South West resort at 2143. The set then works as the empty stock at 2158 (5V60) to the carriage sidings for servicing. Additional trains on a Saturday include a York to Penzance and Penzance to Leeds. Finally, it is envisaged that in 2017 the depot will undergo some upgrades and expansion to cater for the GWR Hitachi AT300 fleet being introduced as a replacement for the 40-year-old HST fleet.

With the old steam shed in the background, Class 52 D1053 Western Patriarch *waits for its next duty eastbound from Penzance in 1974.* (Rail-Online)

Prior to working the up Night Rivera on March 28, 2012, FGW Class 57 57603 Tintagel Castle is berthed with its stock at Long Rock. (Bernard Mills)

THE DIESEL DEPOT | 77

Privatisation Era

The privatisation of Britain's railways in the mid-1990s remains controversial. Had things been done differently, some of the depots that closed could well have found new lives under different companies.

Railtrack became a separate Government-owned company on April 1, 1994 when the track, signalling and freeholds of stations, other buildings and land were transferred to it. The main diesel depots and works were to be sold as part of the Freight Operating Companies (FOCs). The latter was made up of Trainload Freight (TLF), Rail Express Systems (RES) and Freightliner, which included Railfreight Distribution. In an effort to stimulate greater competition, the TLF business, which had previously been sub-divided and managed by commodity – coal, petroleum, construction and metals – was reformed and then split into three regional companies on April 1, 1994. These were TLF South-East, North-East and West, although they were quickly rebranded Mainline, Loadhaul and Transrail respectively. The accompanying table shows how the depots were split between the three TLF companies and RfD prior to being offered for sale. In February 1996, all three former TLF firms were purchased for a combined total of £225.15m by North & South Railways (N&SR), a company formed by a consortium led by US railroad company Wisconsin Central, in a move that nullified the Government's efforts to stimulate a competitive market.

MAIN PHOTO: Freightliner's Leeds Midland Road Depot opened on July 11, 2003 and has recently benefited from a new maintenance building. The site also has a wheel lathe, which has proved popular with other FOCs and heritage loco owners. (Michael Rhodes)

ABOVE: The former Crewe Diesel Depot used to be home to dozens of locos, notably the Class 47, as illustrated by RES 47587. Crewe remains an important railway centre, with both DRS and Freightliner also having their own facilities there. (Chris Booth)

78 THE DIESEL DEPOT

Privatisation Era

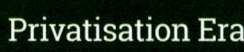

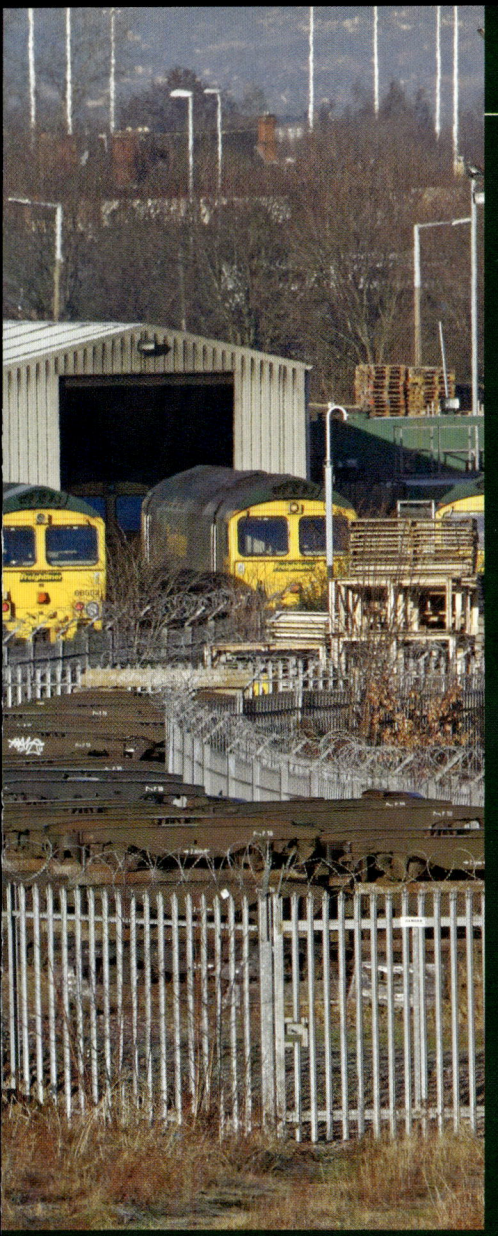

BR Freight Locomotive Depot Privatisation – April 1994

	TFL North East (Loadhaul)	TFL West (Transrail)	TFL South East (Mainline)	RdF
Locos	33 x 37/0	16 x 20	42 x 31	Circa 140 x 47s
	3 x 37/3	101 x 31	25 x 33	
	6 x 37/3	56 x 37/0	60 x 37/0	
	25 x 37/5	1 x 37/3	9 x 37/3	
	16 x 37/7	28 x 37/4	3 x 37/5	
	20 x 47	24 x 37/5	10 x 37/7	
	74 x 56	18 x 37/7	20 x 47	
	33 x 60	6 x 37/9	50 x 58	
		22 x 47	33 x 60	
		57 x 56	25 x 73/1	
		34 x 60		
Super Depot	Immingham	Cardiff Canton	Toton	Tinsley
Main line allocation	Thornaby	Crewe Diesel	Stewarts Lane	Crewe Electric
		Bescot	Stratford	
Shunters only	Doncaster Carr	Springs Branch	Eastleigh	Allerton
	Knottingley	Ayr	Selhurst	
		St Blazey	Old Oak Common	
		Carlisle Upperby		
No allocation	Healey Mills	Millerhill	Hither Green	Saltley
	Blyth Cambois	Perth	Leicester	Ipswich
	Sunderland South Dock	Margam	Peterborough	
		Buxton	Shirebrook	
		Chester	Didcot	
		Motherwell		
Wagons	York	Gloucester		
	Tyne Yard	Burton		
		Duddeston		
		Carnforth		

Note: locomotive figures were proposals and final composition may have differed slightly.

Privatisation Era

Margam Depot in South Wales could be guaranteed to provide plenty of traction during the 1980s. From left to right in this July 23, 1983 image are 47087, 08361, 47246, 37247, 45064 and 47066. The depot officially closed on August 1, 2009. (Michael Rhodes)

well, but none of the individual TOCs and FOCs could support it and demolition came in April 2016. Tinsley and Shirebrook were closed in 1998, with Tinsley being almost immediately bulldozed and Shirebrook going on to see use as a plastics factory. With EWS able to close, mothball or flatten facilities, new entrants to the freight and loco hire market have been forced to convert other buildings or build new facilities.

Pete Waterman had formed LNWR in 1993 and from 1999 he used buildings at Crewe to offer TOCs loco and rolling stock maintenance facilities. In 1994 National Power purchased a single Class 59/2 in order to assess the viability of running its own trains between collieries and limestone quarries to its power stations. A further five Class 59/2s followed in 1995 and in order to service and maintain the fleet it built a depot at Ferrybridge. Sensing that such a move by a new open access operator could be the start of a serious competitor, EWS bought the FOC and its fleet in April 1998.

As Freightliner expanded into the heavy haulage business in 1999, so did its loco servicing and maintenance requirements. It opened a new servicing depot at Earles Sidings and on July 11, 2003 Leeds Midland Road Depot. Also opened at the time was its Southampton Maritime Depot, converted from a former wagon shop that originated around 1996. Ironically, the rise of the publicly owned Direct Rail Services (DRS) was one of the success stories of privatisation. From its core business of transporting nuclear fuel wagons it quickly grew, and in 1999 took over the derelict Carlisle Kingmoor Depot. The four-track shed had opened in 1968 and BR closed it in July 1988. DRS stripped it back to its metal frame and completely re-clad it in corrugated sheeting for its re-opening in July 1999.

The same year saw the launch of GB Railfreight and its rapid growth has seen it open several new depots. In 2001 it converted the former 1987 BR overhead line maintenance depot at New England Peterborough to create a new one-track depot. The re-opening of Whitemoor yard as a Network Rail infrastructure facility saw GBRf initially employing locos from Peterborough until April 18, 2008 when it opened a new depot utilising the former Victorian goods shed building near March station. Electro-Motive Services International (EMSI) had a five-year contract to maintain ten GBRf Class 66s utilising the depot, and an on-call 24-hour 'roaming repairer', ie 'a man in a van'.

With EMSI being part of Electro-Motive Diesel group that manufactured the Class 66s, the depot gave it the ability to address overall maintenance efficiency of the class and maximise GBRf's competitiveness through increased availability of its fleet. The building was converted into a well-equipped diesel depot and engineering facility with space for two locos for exams along with on-site stabling space for six more. The depot is capable of carrying out weekly 'RS' exams, which are regular maintenance checks that take three to four hours to complete, including the replacement of consumable items such as oil filters and exams up to level C, where all safety systems including Driver Safety Devices, AWS and brakes are inspected and tested.

On the passenger side, what few locos were needed for hauled trains were supplied by the FOCs. The growing market for spot hire and special trains meant that in 1998 the decision was taken not to re-open the steam museum at Carnforth. Instead it became a main line depot again and two additional buildings were opened in 2007, operated by West Coast Railways. Fragonset Railways was one of the larger spot hire companies in the 2000s, but its lack of a proper depot, and financial problems, eventually led it to collapse. In 2009, Network Rail opened a new single-track depot at Shrewsbury Coleham Yard for the servicing of its four Class 97s, which were used as pilot locos for the ERTMS re-signalling works on the Cambrian line. The round-topped building resembles a Second World War Nissen hut and holds only one loco.

DB Cargo's rationalisation

As Freightliner Heavy Haul and GBRf especially won increasing amounts of traffic from EWS, the company sought to rationalise and economise wherever possible.

The former EWS depot at Leicester is now used by UK Rail Leasing as a maintenance base, but can also supply fuel to locos requiring it. (UKRL/Phil Marsh)

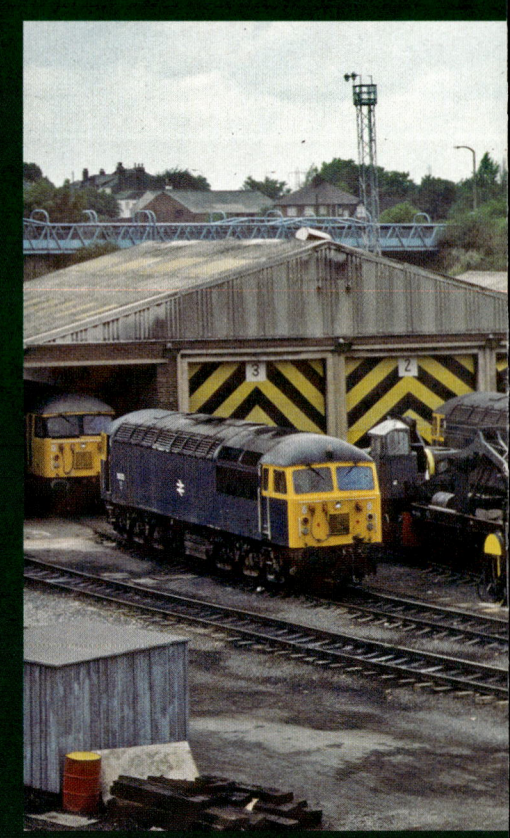

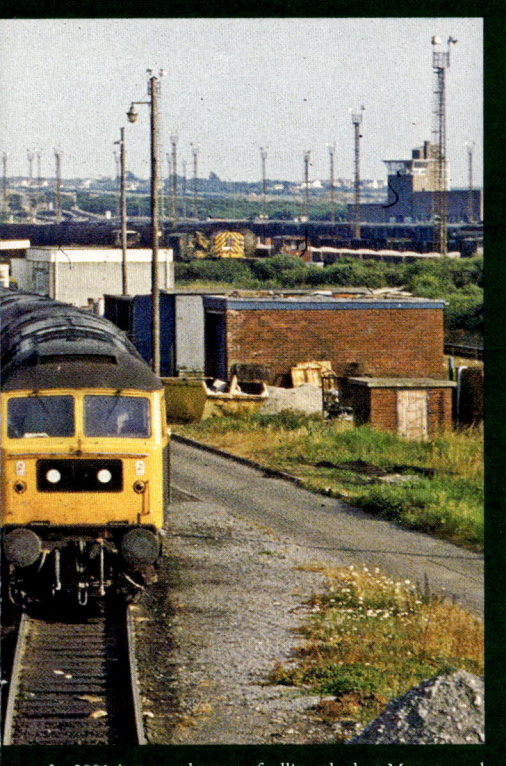

Privatisation Era

Saltley soldiered on after privatisation under RfD, but without a loco allocation. The servicing shed was demolished in 2000 and loco stabling ceased five years later. Class 58s 58018, 58019, 58026, 58029 and 58035 await their next duties on June 15, 1985. (Michael Rhodes)

In 2001 it opened a new fuelling shed at Mountsorrel near Leicester. The structure covered one track and was little more than a glorified car port – but at least it kept the rain off and it reduced light engine movements to Leicester Depot. In 2001, EWS commenced a contract to service Virgin CrossCountry Class 220/221s at Eastleigh, Bristol Barton Hill, Newcastle, Old Oak Common and Three Bridges.

After a period of use as a shunter repair facility, EWS closed the former National Power depot at Ferrybridge along with Crewe in 2003. The once massive facility at Cardiff Canton was run down and EWS closed its doors in May 2004, with many of its staff moving to Margam. However, Pullman Rail ran the site and in May 2012 it was purchased by Colas Rail. On April 24, 2005 Saltley Depot outlived its usefulness and was closed by EWS, with maintenance and fuelling being transferred to Bescot. In December 2007, the final driver signed on at Thornaby Depot before staff were moved into the nearby Tees yard. Locos fuelled at the depot for a little while longer before total closure and demolition.

In November 2008, LNWR at Crewe was sold to Arriva UK Trains, a division of Arriva plc, which is owned by Deutsche Bahn. Following a restructure, DB Schenker's facilities in Newcastle, Cambridge, Eastleigh and Bristol became part of what is now Arriva TrainCare, alongside the pre-existing Crewe facility. The five Arriva TrainCare depots directly employ around 200 staff and have workshop space for more than 70 vehicles. All five offer fuelling and overnight servicing along with heavy lifting of locos and rolling stock, painting and roof access, Ultrasonic Axle Testing (UAT) and all Non-destructive testing (NDT), while Bristol, Eastleigh and Crewe provide vehicle overhaul and refurbishment, with the latter also having a Tandem Wheel Lathe. These services are available to TOCs, FOCs, ROSCOs and train manufacturers.

On November 13, 2007 DB Schenker bought EWS, but its declining fortunes continued. Margam Depot officially closed on August 1, 2009 with loco servicing moving to Margam Knuckle Yard. A new depot was opened at Bescot when the old building was closed in November 2014, and two weeks later a two-road building looking like an 'Anderson Shelter' was opened on the old depot site. Immingham was reduced to a mere fuelling point and the near total collapse of the coal to power station market meant that Worksop closed in October 2015. DB Schenker was rebranded as DB Cargo UK on March 2, 2016.

20 years of privatisation

The highly fragmented UK rail industry is a hugely competitive world. When the Conservative government of the day acquiesced to Wisconsin Central's assertion that the rail industry was in competition with the road industry and not itself, it gave EWS (as it became) a competitive advantage through owning nearly all of the non-passenger depots. Over the ensuing two decades the likes of Freightliner, GBRf, Colas, DRS, other independent operators and maintenance providers have all made substantial gains, with each opening new depots, proving that while the great days of the diesel depot are a fond memory, there's still plenty of variety and interest to be had.

Knottingley was once a major hub for the Yorkshire coal mine/power station circuit. Home to Class 47s, then Class 56s and Class 60s, the depot lost its significance with the closure of the nearby collieries, with imported coal being delivered to the power stations from various ports around the UK. This photo, taken on July 17, 1984, shows 56124, 56073, 56011, 56112 and 56086 (l-r). (Michael Rhodes)

THE DIESEL DEPOT | 81

Carlisle Kingmoor

Carlisle Kingmoor

The railways around Carlisle have a rich heritage of competing companies, duplicate yards and engine sheds. The former Caledonian Railway company opened a steam shed at Kingmoor in 1876 and it was later rebuilt in 1916. The steam shed first saw allocated diesel locomotives in January 1937 when LMS 0-6-0 diesel-electric shunters 7064/5/6/7/8 arrived. Although a couple of that group soon left, they were joined by 7070/1/2/3/4 between March and August 1939.

War and Austerity

However, with the outbreak of World War Two these locomotives were requisitioned by the War Department and they were sent abroad, notably to France and Egypt, and this left Kingmoor devoid of any diesels.

In March 1942, 7110/1/2 came to the depot, followed by 7113/4/5 in May. These locos were used in the yards around Carlisle, of which there were once nine. The

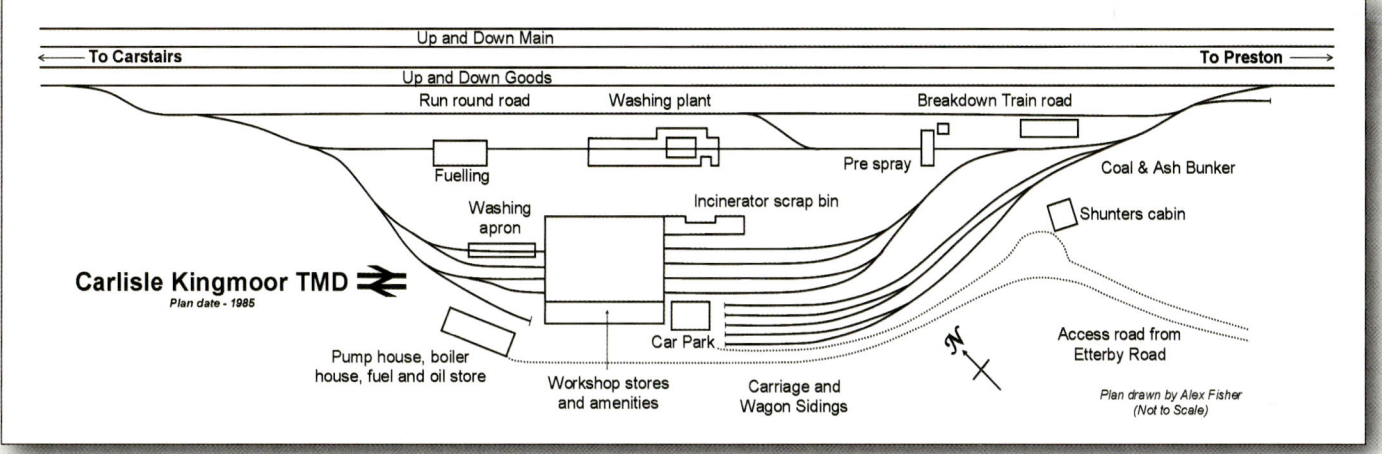

Carlisle Kingmoor

With the West Coast Main line to the right. 25196, 26026, 27066, two more Class 25s, a Class 37 and a pair of Class 85s await events at Kingmoor New Yard depot on July 18, 1984. (Michael Rhodes)

Carlisle Kingmoor TMD
Plan date - 1985

- To Carstairs / To Preston
- Up and Down Main
- Up and Down Goods
- Run round road
- Washing plant
- Breakdown Train road
- Fuelling
- Pre spray
- Coal & Ash Bunker
- Washing apron
- Incinerator scrap bin
- Shunters cabin
- Pump house, boiler house, fuel and oil store
- Car Park
- Access road from Etterby Road
- Workshop stores and amenities
- Carriage and Wagon Sidings

Plan drawn by Alex Fisher (Not to Scale)

THE DIESEL DEPOT | 83

Carlisle Kingmoor

Green liveried English electric Type 4 D306 at Kingmoor on October 8, 1967. (Rail-Online)

British Rail/Sulzer Type 2 D5177 stands at the steam depot's fuel point on August 7, 1965. (Colour-Rail/D Forsyth)

Metrovick Co-Bo D5706, sporting its 12C Barrow-in-Furness shed code graces the new diesel depot in early 1968. The old steam shed can be seen across the main line in the background. (Rail-Online)

Class/Type allocation	
Class	Period
LMS Shunter	January 1937 – December 1939, March 1942 – November 1954
Hudswell Clark	January 1967 – April 1967
03	June 1967 – January 1968
04	May 1967 – January 1968
08	December 1958 – Jul 1988
09	November 1961 – April 1963, June 1963 – October 1968
11	November 1950 – October 1971
17	August 1967 – June 1968
25	November 1967 – March 1987
27	February 1965 – June 1965
28	February 1968 – June 1968
31	May 1985 – October 1987
40	October 1967 – June 1968, May 1973 – October 1987
47	September 1985 – October 1987

shed code reverted to 12A, while December 1958 saw the first Class 08s allocated to Kingmoor steam shed. They were D3565/6/7, which were all new to the depot.

Diesel era

On August 3, 1960, amongst a total of 78 locomotives, Kingmoor steam shed had Class 11s 12085, 12087, and Class 08s D3171, D3566, D3170. On the same day, Carlisle Upperby hosted (Class 44) D5 and D6, which had been allocated to the depot since May 1960 along with Liverpool Edge Hill-based (Class 40) D234. In the early 1960s Upperby often housed three or four Type 4 locos, while November 1961 saw Kingmoor's first Class 09 arrive, in the shape of D4106. Dieselisation of the Carlisle area was proving a slow process, although June 24, 1962 found Class 45s D49, D50, D110 and D150 on Kingmoor, among 83 locos.

Kingmoor hosted Derby-allocated D94 amongst its usual collection of 0-6-0 diesels on June 9, 1963, including 12085, D3172, D3087, D4107 and D3169. From February to June 1965 the depot was home to a solitary Class 27 No D5414, perhaps for driver training, that had come from, and was later returned to, the Leicester Division. Three Hudswell Clark 0-6-0 shunters, Nos D2513/4/17 were allocated to Kingmoor from January 1967, but they had all left by April 1967. Carlisle Upperby closed to steam on December 12, 1966, although it continued as a diesel depot and even gained seven Class 25s from July 1967 to February 1968 and 17 Class 28s between October 1965 and February 1968.

With Kingmoor Diesel Depot not yet open, the steam depot acquired some main line locos. Class 40s D241/2/7/8/9 were amongst those to arrive in October and November 1967. Joining the Class 40s were the loaning and later permanent transfer of Class 25s D5151/2/3/4/5/6 from Thornaby. From May 1967 to January 1968 two Class 04s (D2209 and D2253) were based at the steam depot along with a solitary Class 03 (D2390) from June 1967 to January 1968. Kingmoor steam depot closed on January 1, 1968 and at the same time the new diesel depot, which had been built on the opposite side of the main line, was opened.

The diesel depot

The diesel depot was a four-road through shed that was designed to maintain diesel electric locomotives, diesel multiple units and coaching stock. With an eye for the future electrification of the West Coast Main Line, the depot required only minimal alterations in order to host electric locos. Each road had a full-length pit, fitted with fluorescent lighting, an air supply and 50-volt electrical points for the use of portable tools and other equipment. There was a mobile crane for heavy lifting of up to 6¼ tons, along with a specially designed straddle crane with

locos spent much of their time out working and on Sunday April 8, 1945 only 7112 was on shed alongside 92 steam engines. 7112 was at Kingmoor until December 1950 when it was transferred to 8C Speke Junction. June 10, 1950 saw the depot's code change from 12A to 68A and in November 1950 four more shunters were allocated to Kingmoor. They were of a type later classified as Class 11 under TOPS and 12080/1/2/3 came to Kingmoor along with 12079 in December 1950. On October 2, 1955 Class 11 No 12080 and Class 08 13170, which was actually allocated to Carlisle Upperby at the time, were on Kingmoor shed. On February 1, 1958 the

Carlisle Kingmoor

a capacity of up to ½ ton that covered all four roads. In order to lift locomotives clear of their bogies, one of the roads had reinforced concrete along its full length. Four 20-ton capacity electrically-powered screw jacks were used and they lifted locos for preventive maintenance and bogie cleaning, etc.

Facilities at the depot were quite comprehensive and there were separate rooms for testing coolant water, lubricating oil and fuel injectors, battery maintenance and filter cleaning, along with a fitter's workshop that had a large store of spare parts. From January 1, 1968 the depot had an allocation of Class 03 D2209/53, Class 08 D2390, D3087, D3169-73, D3283, D3567, D3736/40/1, D4107/56/7, Class 11 12080/3/4/5, Class 17 D8500-20, Class 25 D5151-6, D5248-56, D7549/50/13-6 and Class 40 D241/2/7/8/9, D390/1. With usual prefix of 'ill-fated', an ominous number of 13 Class 28s were transferred from Carlisle Upperby to Kingmoor in February 1968, but by June 1968 they'd all left. Another class that had a brief association with Kingmoor was the 35 Class 17s, which initially came to the steam depot from August 1967. With the opening of the diesel depot they moved over, along with subsequent additional transfers – a process that continued until May 1968. No sooner had the last arrived, however, than they were all transferred away in June 1968 to the Preston Division.

Resident shunter D3172 shares the old steam depot with another example, a British Rail/Sulzer Type 2 and an unidentified steam loco on August 7, 1965. (Colour-Rail/D Forsyth)

From May 1967 to January 1968 two Class 04s (D2209 in blue and D2253 in green) were based at the steam depot, where they were photographed on May 27, 1967. (Rail-Online)

The 1970s

With Class 50s working the northern part of the WCML before electrification, they were regular visitors to the depot before being transferred away to the Western Region in the early 1970s. Resident shunters as of December 31, 1971 were 3087, 3169-73, 3511/30/1/4/65-8/80/1, 3736/40/1/68/84, 4141/2/56. Upon electrification of the line through Carlisle, a single road in the depot was wired and Kingmoor became responsible for performing A and B exams on electric locos, alongside the existing maintenance routines on diesels and DMUs. In May 1973, an influx of 23 Class 40s came to Kingmoor along with 38 Class 25s. When seven more Class 40s arrived in August 1973, Kingmoor was at its height as a diesel depot. On May 6, 1973 the depot gained the TOPS code of 'KM'; on that date its main line allocation was Class 25s 5188-95, 5297/8/9, 7542-53/99, 7626/39/46/51/9 and Class 40s 207-13/36/41/2/3/5/87-90/4-7, 300/1/3.

The 1970s also saw a large number of Class 08s come and go, along with the depot code changing again to 'KD' on January 5, 1975. 84 differently numbered Class 25s were assigned to Kingmoor between December 1974 and May 1986, when the last of the class was transferred away. During 1976 the depot was home to several withdrawn Class 24s. Rivalling the variation in the number of Class 25 seen at the depot were the 70 Class 40s based there between December 1974 and February 8, 1985 when 40012 *Aureol* was withdrawn; although, it later went to work as a Class 97 on the Crewe Station engineering works before being preserved. Showing the variety of electric locos that could be found at Kingmoor is this tally from the late Friday evening of September 4, 1981, when alongside the usual 08s, 25, 40 and 47s were 81005, 83015, 85018, 86001 and 87022.

Allocation January 1, 1982

Class 08	08078/104-7/396/450/2/601/759/844/910-12
Class 25	25036/44/56/62/84/5/97/140/6/9/91/200-2/18/36/322
Class 40	40001/2/8/12/20/2/60/101/26/38/54/8/62

Changing times

In April 1983 Kingmoor gained what was perhaps its most famous resident: Class 40 40122, the erstwhile D200 and pioneer of the English Electric design. It was withdrawn in 1981, but thanks to a railway magazine's enthusiast appeal and the hard work of Toton's apprentices, it was put back into traffic and based at Kingmoor. The loco went on to work a variety of specials and was a regular from Carlisle on the out and back passenger services to Leeds.

With the introduction of Class 31s on local services from Leeds along the Settle line to Carlisle, Kingmoor

Clayton Type 1 D8508 was transferred to Kingmoor around the time this image was taken, on October 8, 1967. It was delivered new to Polmadie on October 30, 1967 after it returned to the Scottish depot in May 1969 after spending 11 months based at Preston. (Rail-Online)

THE DIESEL DEPOT | 85

Carlisle Kingmoor

A line up of first-generation DMUs at Kingmoor on July 10, 1978. Among the Class 108s, including M50956 to the right, is a route learning 'bubble car'. (Michael Rhodes)

KD Snapshots

Sunday July 5, 1964

BR Type 4	D11 D107
EE Type 4	D264
Shunters	D3169, D3170, D3171, D3172, D3173, D3567, D4107, 12083, 12084, 12085
EE Type 1	D8122, D8127
BR Type 2	D5197

Friday March 6, 1981 (2205)

Class 08	08419 08601 08759
Class 25	25120 25172 25233
Class 40	40017 40137
Class 47	47102 47345
Class 81	81012
Class 82	82008
Class 85	85033
Class 86	86010

Saturday May 2, 1981 (0015)

Class 08	08105 08107 08450
Class 25	25038 25065 25168 25246
Class 40	40008 40025 40135
Class 45	45034
Class 47	47421 47579
Class 81	81013 81015 81021

Friday May 7, 1982 (2305)

Class 08	08105 08107 08450 08677 08910
Class 25	25057 25140 25167 25208 25259 25307
Class 40	40034 40129 40185
DMU	M50951 M50959 M50962 M50963 M50967 M50969 M50982 M50987, M56235 M56240 M56243 M56245 M56246 M56250 M56252 M56263 M56270

Thursday April 12, 1984 (2005)

Class 08	08078 08105 08601
Class 25	25325 25327
Class 40	40090
DMU	M53116 M53435 M53498 M53950 M53952 M53953 M53954 M53957 M54227 M54236 M54242 M54244 M54265

Monday September 16, 1985 (1420)

Class 08	08826
Class 25	25196 25198 25300 25302 25303
DMU	53950 53958 53966 53969 53976 53980 53982 54224 54227 54239 54246 54249 54252 54256 DB975042

commenced servicing the type in 1984. That year also saw the closure of the fuel and inspection depot situated in Kingmoor Yard. Henceforth locos would travel to Kingmoor for fuelling and any maintenance required. May 1985 saw four Class 31s based at Kingmoor, and a visit to the depot on April 27, 1986 found 08602, 25051/178/254/325, 31209, 40001 and 47119/200/339/451/78 along with 18 DMU cars. 31209 had been assigned to the depot from September 1985 and was there for exactly a year, one of 19 Class 31s until the last three (31270/1/5) left in October 1987.

In perhaps what may be considered the depot's 'Indian Summer', a tranche of 30 Class 47s was allocated to KD. At the time, a weekday at the depot would see maintenance undertaken on around 35 main line electrics and diesels, six shunters, and 36 DMUs, along with coaching stock vehicles. There was an automatic washing plant with a built-in lubricating oil and storage area, which catered for locos and passenger coaches together. For carriage servicing the depot had five maintenance lines that had a variety of ancillary services including a specially designed effluent plant to chemically treat any spilt oil before it could enter the drainage system.

The depot also had a 75-ton steam crane available 24 hours a day to deal with any incidents in the Carlisle area. To administer all of these capabilities the depot had a two-storey amenity block incorporated within the main building. It provided staff facilities for the 135 men on shift work as well as two well-equipped Lecture Rooms for training apprentices, maintenance staff and footplate men.

Traffic decline

In the mid-1980s Kingmoor Yard was only seeing 16 daily WCML Speedlink freights, along with a handful of Trip freights. The dramatic fall in traffic around Carlisle meant that the need for the depot had ebbed away and although more Class 47s had joined the original 30, October 1987 saw Kingsmoor's main line allocation transferred away. By that time there were only 19 Class 47s on its books, along with Class 40, D200. It was left with several Class 08s, but when the depot closed on July 11, 1988 08485/586/690/768/808/26/27/44/910/1/2 all departed for new homes.

Carlisle still retained a traincrew depot, and in 1993 Trainload Freight noted that it was to continue as a multi-sector traincrew depot, but trimmed to 40 men. However, it so happened that 25% of the 160 men there at the time were due to retire within four years.

KD's resurrection

The depot wasn't immediately demolished but lingered on in an increasingly dilapidated state. The 1990s privatisation process brought several new operators into the freight market, and one prominent entrant was Direct Rail Services (DRS). The haulage of nuclear flask traffic had been handled by BR until 1994 when British Nuclear Fuels set up DRS in order to bring the activity in house. For its trains, it initially bought five Class 20/3s, which were refurbished at Brush Traction, Loughborough. As DRS diversified its traffic flows and purchased six Class 37/6s in 1997, space and facilities were restricted at its Sellafield depot, leading it to look further afield.

The derelict Carlisle Kingmoor had survived Railtrack plans to demolish it and sell off the land and this enabled DRS to lease the building in 1998. It began a complete refurbishment of the facilities, including new exterior cladding in DRS colours. The depot's sidings were restored to use, and in May 1999 it reopened. Since then several developments have taken place, including the installation of a sand tower and increased office space. The depot has staged regular open days and is now an integral facility in the maintenance of DRS' loco fleet.

Kingmoor diesel depot on July 18, 1984 with 08569, 25202 and 25044 in attendance. (Michael Rhodes)

2017 Edition OUT NOW!

THE INDISPENSABLE, HANDS-ON REVIEW AND DIRECTORY OF THE UK RAIL INDUSTRY

Edited by *Modern Railways'* Ken Cordner, with contributions from Roger Ford, Tony Miles, Alan Williams and other members of the team, *The Modern Railway 2017* hardback runs to 208 pages and provides an in-depth examination of:
- Policy and finance
- Infrastructure maintenance and renewal
- Train operation (passenger and freight)
- Key projects now under way
- Rolling stock manufacturing and maintenance
- Signal and telecommunications
- Customer interface and support
- Light rail and Metro systems
- European developments

Over 2600 Rail Companies listed!

Special features include:
- 2017 - Year of Recovery. *Modern Railways'* Roger Ford on why 2017 is a key year for major rail projects
- Record train orders pose delivery challenge – Roger Ford's annual rolling stock review looks at the effects of policy shifts on new train deliveries
- Crossings at a crossroads? Modern Railways columnist Alan Williams examines concerns over level crossings as the railway gets faster and busier
- Profits and performance at train operating companies – specialist analysis
- Seismic changes in rail freight – our annual freight sector review charts a course to recovery
- Electrification gets into gear – Roger Ford examines the challenges of managing delivery and costs
- Into Europe – major projects, modernisation and new technology on the continent's railways
- Profiles of all the main players in today's UK rail industry – from multinationals to innovative start-ups.

The most comprehensive directory of UK rail companies

As well as editorial coverage of all the main players and projects, *The Modern Railway 2017* includes a comprehensive directory of over 2,600 suppliers and businesses involved in keeping the UK industry in operation. This section has comprehensive contact information including web addresses and email details, making this publication an essential tool for the railway professional.

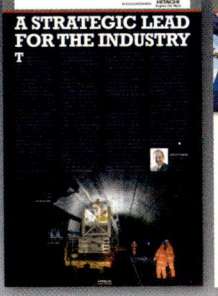

The Modern Railway sponsored by
HITACHI Inspire the Next

JUST £25.00 PLUS FREE P&P*

*Free 2nd class P&P on all UK & BFPO orders. Overseas charges apply.

Free P&P* when you order online at www.keypublishing.com/shop

OR

Call UK: 01780 480404
Overseas: +44 1780 480404
Monday to Friday 9am-5:30pm

1253/16

SUBSCRIBERS SAVE 20% - CALL FOR YOUR DISCOUNT!

Stratford Open Day 1983

Stratford Open Day 1983

Adrian Willats attended the open day at the sprawling East London Depot and Works and was delighted at the variety of exhibits on display.

ABOVE: Bright yellow London Transport battery loco L61 was among the colourful exhibits at the 1983 Stratford Open Day. (All photos Adrian Willats)

BELOW: Resident Class 08 08531, complete with information board, stands adjacent to the servicing shed.

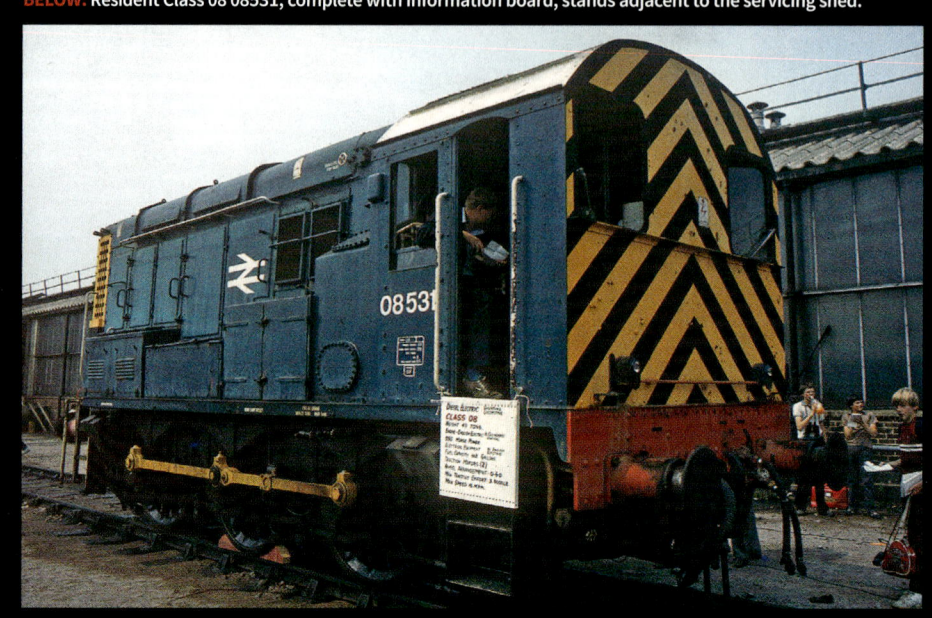

Open days at depots and railway workshops were familiar events during the 1970s and 80s in particular. They provided the perfect opportunity for enthusiasts and photographers to gain access to places that were normally 'off limits', and were guaranteed to produce a wide variety of rolling stock.

It was a pleasant Saturday July 9 that saw the traditional open day crowds heading for a well-known east London location, no doubt encouraged by the good weather that my slides suggest was enjoyed. As was to be expected back then, a wide range of locomotives, multiple units, coaches and engineering vehicles were on display. Some of them were inside the depot buildings, including 47006 that was suspended (bogieless) from a large crane. Others were arranged outside, usually with reasonable space for photography and ready to be prodded, poked and climbed on by younger visitors. I don't recall the practice of getting a souvenir 'snap' of people in front of a loco being all that common back then, but I'm sure that it is much more widespread now due in no small part to the rise of the mobile phone. It's also hard to believe, but the souvenir programme was only 40p!

I only took 20 slides during the day, but looking through the subjects I chose gives an interesting perspective on what was still considered 'everyday' more than 30 years ago, together with the new developments

Stratford Open Day 1983

ABOVE: At the time the Mk 3 sleeper was ushering in a more refined overnight experience as it replaced the elderly Mk 1 equivalent.

BELOW: Complete with white roof and silver buffers, a Class 105 Cravens unit inside the DMU servicing shed.

ABOVE: Peak 46044 awaits attention inside Stratford Works. The workshops performed various repairs and overhauls, and were also responsible for stripping useable parts from withdrawn locos from time to time.

BELOW: A power car from HST set 254035 stands outside the servicing shed.

represented by two of the exhibits. For example, Class 105 DMUs in overall blue were still in widespread use; indeed, my friend Robert and I were to become very familiar with them two years later on our East Anglian Golden Rail holiday. Late evening journeys back from Norwich to our base in Great Yarmouth featured steamed up windows and seemingly every part of the unit constantly vibrating or rattling! Such things would have the rail travellers of the 21st century reaching for their phones to fire off complaining emails, but as railway enthusiasts back then? Well, what do you think – WE LOVED IT! Those hard-working products of the Cravens factory also remind me of our first visit to North Woolwich in 1984, for it was one of those units that got us there. What you might call Stratford 'low level' was in the open air back then, just think of how that site looks now and all the different types of train that have passed over the tracks since.

Representing the new 'age of the train' for the early 1980s were a Class 58 freight loco and a Mk 3 sleeping car, the first examples of both having been built only the previous year. Sadly, today only the sleepers remain in use, and in much reduced numbers. The last Class 58s were withdrawn 15 years ago. I do have a vague recollection of having some of our lunch in a Class 315 EMU, but perhaps memory is teasing me again and that may have been another open day, as it certainly doesn't seem to be visible in any of my slides.

As often happened with British Rail open days, at least those in greater London, some London Transport exhibits were on show. On this occasion they included yellow liveried battery locomotive L61, part of LT's engineering stock. A Class 254 High Speed Train power car was also present, along with the Ultrasonic Test Train DB975007 and DB975008, and 25177 that was used to perform re-railing demonstrations.

BELOW: Although its doors were secured shut, that didn't stop youngsters from climbing all over brand new 58002.

THE DIESEL DEPOT | 89

Cardiff Canton

Cardiff Canton

In the diesel era Cardiff Canton was one of the UK's largest depots but, like Tinsley and Crewe, the traffic for which it was built has largely gone. As locomotives disappeared, so too did a once-proud staff who called Cardiff Canton their home. The shields and cups won by Canton's first aid team are long gone, as are the trophies for football, darts and snooker that were won by a workforce whose camaraderie transcended that of the mere workplace.

Canton in steam

A six-road 240ft long locomotive shed was opened in June 1882, and extended in 1897, and a 28-road roundhouse with a 55ft diameter turntable added. In 1925 a new coaling stage and loco lifting and repair shed were built. A replacement 65ft diameter turntable was installed in 1931 at the west end of the yard to accommodate larger locos. During those halcyon days of the GWR, the depot had a complement of 120 locos: 30 shunters and small tank engines, 40 heavy goods/mineral locos and 50 main line passenger engines. Under the 1950 shed code system, Newport, Ebbw Junction was 86A and Cardiff Canton was 86C, before becoming 88A from 1961 to 1963 and finally usurping Newport, Ebbw Junction to become 86A from 1963.

The first diesels

Multiple units came to Canton in 1959, with part of the steam shed converted to accommodate them. The first allocated main line diesel was Bayer Peacock Hymek D7022 in February 1962. Closure to steam came on September 8, 1962 and Cardiff East Dock shed, which had lost its loco allocation in 1958, inherited all of Canton's steam fleet, including Castles, Halls, Granges and Manors. The steam shed was soon demolished, except for the large water tank at the east end of the yard and part of the 1882 building that was retained to form a new diesel servicing shed.

As more Hymeks arrived in December 1962, Nos 7057-60 took over the heavy steel coil trains from Margam Abbey steelworks and Trostre and Velindre strip mills. Six Westerns (D1012/3/4/44/5/9) came in December 1962, sharing the aforementioned duties with the Hymeks. The Westerns were also used on the Margam and Trostre plant steel and coal trains on diagrams that took them as far afield as London, as they gradually replaced the Class 42XX tanks.

Diesel Electrics replace Diesel Hydraulics

By October 1963 50 Westerns out of the 74-strong class had spent some time allocated to Canton. Most left in the following year and when D1007/8/11/2/4/6/7/8/22/23/25/6/37/8/40/2 departed in April 1964, they had all

ABOVE: It's Christmas 1978 and dozens of locos sit out the festive period waiting to return to work. The larger maintenance building is on the left and the servicing shed to its right. (All photos Michael Rhodes)

Cardiff Canton TMD
Plan date - 1965

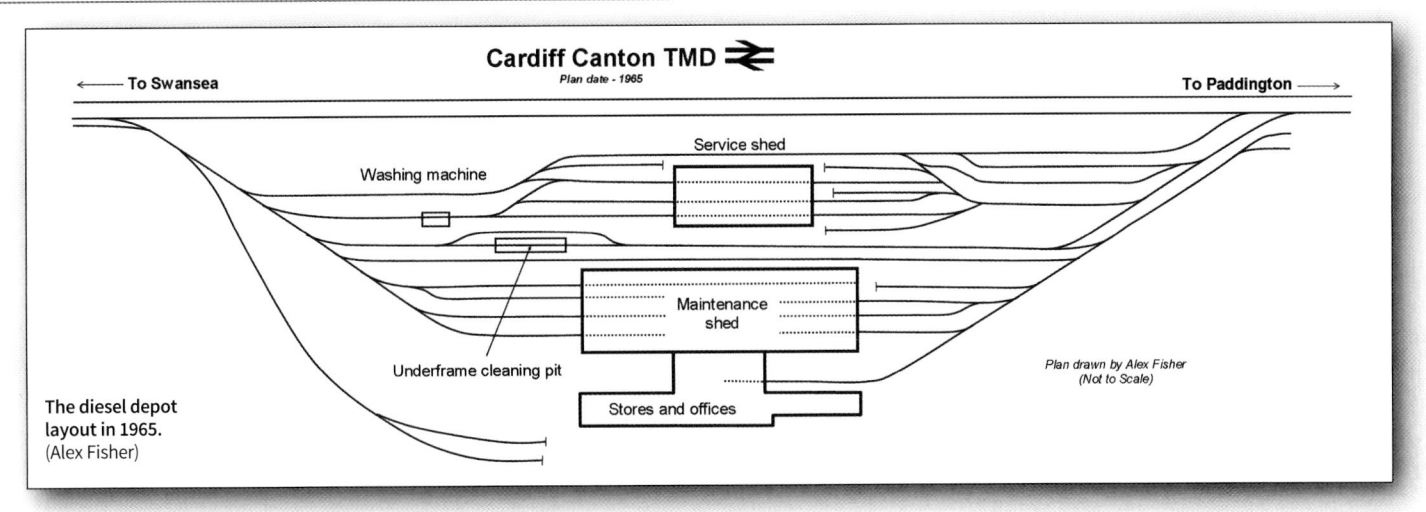

The diesel depot layout in 1965.
(Alex Fisher)

Plan drawn by Alex Fisher
(Not to Scale)

gone. By 1970 77 Hymeks had spent at least some time allocated to Canton, but their ranks also dwindled as they were replaced by a vast influx of Class 37s and Class 47s. After two ER Class 37s were loaned for trials on the South Wales Valleys, the first to be based at Canton was D6742 in September 1962, followed by D6743 in the October. In all, 160 Class 37s received a Canton allocation between 1963 and 1974, including D6600-8/6742/3/6819-79/81/2/85/6/9/91-6927/9-6999 and 37228. A colossal 176 Class 47s alone were assigned to Canton prior to 1974. The depot had no shunting engines in its early years and instead 46 of what became Class 08s went to nearby Cathays en masse, along with six GWR diesel shunters, 15101-6. Most of the 08s had come new to either Llanelly or Duffryn Yard in 1956 and had moved from there to Cardiff East Dock before transferring to Cardiff Cathays in October 1962. In November 1964 the six GWR shunters and 44 Class 08s were moved again, mainly to

Cardiff Canton

ABOVE: Three Class 47s in the main maintenance building in 1978.

BELOW: With the diesel hydraulic era almost at an end in this 1976 image, a Class 52 Western shares the stabling roads outside the servicing shed with a pair of Class 31s.

Cardiff Canton, so Cathays was left with none. From November to December 1964 a single diesel mechanical shunter, D2128 (later Class 03), was allocated to the depot. May to June 1965 also saw the brief return of D8069 from Tinsley, no doubt in connection with the introduction of the type through South Yorkshire to South Wales coal and steel workings. Another allocation of a single locomotive type was Peak 45058 from December 1976 to January 1977. More numerous, however, were the 22 Class 46s that were based at Canton between May 1975 and May 1977. A further pair of Class 20s (20179 and 20201) had brief stays in May 1979.

The rapid dieselisation of the Cardiff Division saw main line loco numbers rise from 29 at the end of 1962 to 236 by the end of August 1964. Steam locos were culled from 1,111 to 367 during the same period and 14 steam sheds had been closed by November 1964. The division had hoped to rid itself of steam by the end of 1964, but the protracted delivery of the Swindon-built 650hp Type 1 diesel-hydraulics (Class 14) meant that it was spring 1965 before such an aspiration could become a reality. It was already recognised at that time that Canton, apart from the depot's 43 Class 14s, would concentrate on diesel-electric loco comprising 197 Class 47s, 120 Class 37s, 62 shunters and 96 DMUs. Canton's last Class 14 was D9514, withdrawn in April 1969. With the Westerns already gone, the first of 35 Class 25s came to Canton in May 1972 to help expedite the demise of the Hymeks, the final two being D7093 and D7098 in December 1972. The former was reallocated to Bristol Bath Road, and with D7098's withdrawal, the depot no longer had any diesel-hydraulics – they were concentrated on the West of England main line.

The new Diesel Depot

In the winter of 1962/63 contractor Kyle Stewart was tasked with building a new diesel maintenance depot on the 30-acre site, at a cost of £1,324,000. The Rt Hon Lord Brecon (Minister of State for Welsh Affairs) opened the facility on September 18, 1964 with Canton claiming to be the best equipped in Europe. The staff complement shortly after opening was: 40 managers and supervisors, 31 clerical staff, 382 maintenance fitters and 55 unskilled men. They were entrusted with around 360 locos for major maintenance, 197 for normal maintenance and 62 shunting engines. Finally, with a view to catering for future traffic increases, the depot was designed to cope with the daily servicing of 99 main line locos.

The depot comprised of a main servicing shed, complemented by a wheel lathe shop and an 800ft-long DMU shed. The three-road servicing facility, converted from the former steam shed, was 270ft long by 81ft wide and came into use in October 1963. It could hold nine locos, three on each road. Six of the nine available berths had fluorescently lit inspection pits, and one also had side pits. There were 12 men based at the servicing shed, classed variously as labourers, fitter's mates, semi-skilled and skilled fitters, Chargehand and Movements Supervisor.

Arriving locos would predominantly come through the washing plant and enter the shed from the west end. They would then be assessed by the Movements Supervisor to determine whether a fuelling and service check or A/B exam was required. Lubricating oil, coolant and fuel were pumped to the shed, while brake blocks and sand were requisitioned from the stores department. The servicing

The late 1990s, although BR sectorisation liveries still dominate with a blue Class 56, two Transrail Class 37s and a 'Dutch' liveried example.

Cardiff Canton

Shunter duties May 1987	
1 DB	Cardiff Canton Carriage Shed
2 DB	Cardiff Central Station Pilot
1	Cardiff Roath Dock (North Side)
1	Newport Docks
2 DB	Cardiff Tidal
1 DB	Radyr Junction
1 DB	Cathays Carriage and Wagon Works
1 AB	Barry Docks/Cadoxton Yard
1 DB	National Smokeless Fuels Abercwmboi Phurnacite Works
1 DB	East Usk Junction Sorting Sidings
1 DB	East Usk Junction Sorting Sidings and trips to BSC Llanwern/Uskmouth Power Station/Alpha Steel Works and trips between Maindee Bank Engineers Yard/Godfrey Road/Alexandra Dock Junction Sidings and BSC Llanwern/Newport Docks
1 DB	Severn Tunnel Junction Down Yard, South Side of line
1 DB	Severn Tunnel Junction Down Yard, South Side of line (afternoons and nights only)
2 DB	Bristol Yard (Up side) North side of Mainline
1 DB	Transfer Pilot
1 DB	Hereford Yard

DB = Dual Braked; AB = Air Braked

Additional Class 08s on external hire	
2	National Smokeless Fuels Abercwmboi Phurnacite Works
1	British Coal Merthyr Vale Colliery
	BC Deep Navigation Colliery Bridgend
	Rafyr RCE Yard
	BSC Llanwern Works
	Machen Quarry

ABOVE: A single Class 47, a DMU and some hauled stock in the carriage shed in March 1977.

BELOW: One of the roads in the maintenance building was equipped with eight lifting jacks to enable bogie changes and work on traction motors to take place.

shed undertook the majority of the B exams, which in effect made it a Level 2 depot in its own right. After servicing, locos would leave from the east end either to the holding sidings or directly into traffic.

The main shed was 360ft by 92ft and had one through road, with dead end roads at each end, making a total of seven. Inside the depot there were power and compressed air points for dispensing lubricating oils, steam and water. Dirty oil was removed via pipes to a collecting tank outside the shed. Four exhaust steam pipes were available to disperse to atmosphere steam from loco train-heating boilers stabled on any one of the ten berths. A 10 ton capacity overhead crane spanned each end of the shed, this being a product of the original planning when the Western Region was weighted towards diesel hydraulics. It wasn't strong enough to lift the largest engine and generator sets of the region's main line diesel-electrics.

In the centre of the depot was a workshop area with adjacent stands for spare engine parts and transmissions. The stores were sited on the south side and had rooms for clothing, fitting, first aid, charts, clean working and filter cleaning. The clean room was subdivided into two parts, one for the testing of fuel injectors and the other for testing lubricating oils and engine coolant. The main shed undertook occasional B exams, heavy repairs and also C to E exams. Two locos could be berthed on four of the dead-end roads, while the other two would accept a single loco and shunter or three shunters. At the west end of the main shed, road seven had eight Maschinenfabrik Geiger 25 ton jacks for lifting locos to enable wheel set and traction motor changes. Additionally, power unit swaps could be done with a 40 ton electrically operated hoist situated outside the west end of the main shed over roads seven and eight. To test the power units, Canton had a 3,000hp capacity load bank, which meant that when the Class 56s came, they could be tested up to their full output rating. The depot also had a group of men tasked with looking after the maintenance equipment, obviating the need for a poor workman to blame his tools.

The 1970s and 1980s

With the introduction of TOPS in 1973, Cardiff's depot code became 'CF'. Making up for its lack of an early association with Class 08s were the 123 (12% of the 996-strong class) different 'Gronks' that called Canton home between 1974 and 1998. The last Class 25s left Canton in November 1977, however the 1970s and 80s really belonged to the 37s and 47s. Between 1974 and 1998 310

A typical 1980s scene at Canton with two Peaks, a Class 56, two Class 31s and a Class 47 visible.

THE DIESEL DEPOT | 93

Cardiff Canton

ABOVE: Two Peaks (45057 and 46016) and two Class 47s inside the servicing shed in 1977.

BELOW: An overall view of the western end of the depot in 1977.

Locomotive Examination Frequencies						
Class	A	B	C	D	E	F
08, 09, 97806	4 weeks	4 months	1 year	2 years	4 years	
37/0, 37/3, 37/4, 37/5, 37/7	55	275	825	1650	4950	
37901-904 (Mirrlees Engine)	100	400	2000	4000		
37905-906 (Ruston Engine)	80	400	1200	3600		7200
47/0, 47/3	55	275	825	1650	4950	9900
56	60	300	1200	3600		7200

Intervals are TOPS hours, except for the shunters as shown.

Class 37s were allocated to Canton. The Class 47s also saw a similarly large number. From July 1979 Class 56s began to usurp the 37s and 47s, although the latter lasted until 1992 and the former until 1998. By December 1979, Class 56s had ousted the triple-headed Class 37s on the 2,740 ton iron ore trains from Port Talbot docks to Llanwern steelworks. Ten Class 56s, 56033/5/7/8/40/1/3/4/5/6, were initially allocated to Canton, while the Class 37s were put to work on MGR trains to Aberthaw power station. In 1988 Canton had 171 resident locos and it was classified a Level 4 depot, meaning it was able to perform exams up to E level. Alongside the 08s were ten Class 09s, 09001/3/8/11/3/5/7/105/7/203, which were based at Canton between June 1988 and the late 1990s.

The 1990s

By 1991 Trainload Steel was sponsoring the depot with 120 resident locos, including 22 Class 08/09s and Classes 37, 47, 56 and 60 across 12 different loco pools. More than 85 locos were for freight and covered Trainload construction, steel, petroleum and coal duties. The rest were for Regional Railways and departmental use. When the Trainload Freight depot diamonds were introduced, Cardiff adopted the Goat and it was applied to locos from RfD, TLF and Infrastructure. One of the first Class 60s to a carry the Cardiff Canton depot insignia was 60037 *Helvellyn*. On July 7, 1993 it was at Canton for repairs, after which it was test run from Cardiff to Margam before being released into traffic the following day.

In the early 1990s the depot's complement of staff were working across three shifts on weekdays, with one early Saturday turn. Staff included 183 unskilled, semi-skilled and skilled men, 18 supervisors and seven managers. As well as the depot engineer and production engineer on the day turn, other positions included a shift production engineer, two supervisors in the main shed, a chargehand in the servicing shed and a movements supervisor. By the start of the 1990s a stores computer system kept track of everything from bolts to traction motors. The system would automatically re-order as appropriate from the National Supply Centre at Doncaster, with road deliveries up to three times a week. After Canton pursued BS 5750 certification its tools were also specially accounted for and calibrated. It also adopted the Rail Vehicle Records System (RAVERS) to make record keeping easier and more accurate.

Testing of electrical equipment was also undertaken. Level 1 involved in-situ testing of gauges and instruments, with level 2 being external testing. Canton's Hegenscheidt-type under-floor wheel lathe was used predominantly by the Trainload Freight locos, along with InterCity HSTs and Class 47s, Parcel Sector locos from Bristol Bath Road, NSE's Reading-based DMU sets and Regional Railway's DMUs from Bristol and Swansea, in addition to those at Canton. BR stock also included the shunters from the Allied Steel and Wire yard at Cardiff Docks, preserved

Allocation December 31, 1968

(Class 47)1584/5/6/8-93/5/7/8/9, 1603/5/6, 1752/3, 1901-27/34/6; (Class 08) 3256-67, 3357/8, 3419-24, 3523/94/5, 3603/4/7, 3747/8/9/53/9, 3807/19/22, 4011/2, 4125-8/70/9; (Class 37) 6600-4, 6875/6/8/9/85/6, 6906/13/21/38/41/3/4/54-8/69-82/4-99; (Class 35) 7018/50-5/63/4/7/70/3-99; Class 14) 9500/2/14/8/27/8/38.

diesels and the privately owned Class 59s. The lathe could turn wheels with or without their being removed. Interestingly, the equipment included a rope haulage system to allow vehicles to be positioned without recourse to the use of a shunting engine.

The depot had two independent snowploughs and sufficient miniature snowploughs to equip eight locos. Large incidents and derailments in the area were dealt with by Canton's breakdown train, which was made up of three coaches carrying re-railing equipment and bunks for the men, along with what was, at the time, the only travelling crane in Wales, a Cowans Sheldon 75 ton capacity example. Smaller derailments and incidents were dealt with using a BRUFF road/rail vehicle, which could carry lighting and jacking equipment along with up to seven men.

Two Class 37s and a Class 60 undergo maintenance at Canton in the late 1990s.

Cardiff Canton

Cardiff Canton Allocation – early 1991

DCWA: Departmental – Western Region Civil Engineer
37010/12/35/38/46/133/38/39/41/42/46/58/74/91/207/21/30/63/64/372

DCWC: Departmental – Western Region Civil Engineer
PWM 97651/53

DOPA: Departmental – Operations Class 09, Sudbrook
97806

FAWK: Freight – Construction, Westbury
56001/31/31/34/47/39/40/41/43/50/51/52/53/55/56

FEKK: Freight – Coal, Trainload, Aberthaw
37701/02/03/04
37796/97/98/99, 800
37801/2/3, 883-7/889/894-9

FHBK: Freight – Coal, Trainload
37689/90/91/95/96/97/98/99

FPEK: Freight – Petroleum South Wales
37072/78/162/220/48/73/80/94/350/71
47094/197/277/318/26/27/81
60026

FMAK: Freight – Steel
37058/97/197/225/54

FMHK: Freight – Steel
37710/11/12/13/14/15/16/17/18/19
37901/02/03/04/05/06

FMSK: Freight
08375/479/81/93/589/652/54/60/64/68/787/804/18/22/35/36/48/932/42
09001/15

FQCK: Freight – Coal, Distribution Network
37235/39
37223
37212/13/15/17/131/67, 274

PCFA: Regional Railways
37408/28/30

Privatisation and rebirth

When the Trainload Freight business was split up into regional companies for selling off, each area had its own 'Super Depot'; Trainload Freight West's (TFW) was Cardiff Canton. The other TFW depots were: Margam, Gloucester, St Blazey, Bescot, Buxton, Wigan Springs Branch, Carlisle Upperby, Motherwell, Millerhill and Ayr. After privatisation in the mid-1990s, the depot became a joint Arriva Trains Wales and English, Welsh and Scottish Railway (EWS) facility. Sixty-seven Class 56s were at some point allocated to Canton, but the continued decline in rail freight saw many moved away or replaced by Class 60s. Forty-eight Class 60s were resident until Type 5 power came to an end when 56010/32/7/44/53/64/73/6/103/1 13/5/9 left in September 1997 along with the remaining Class 60s. In November 1998, the final Class 37s departed Canton, leaving only shunters: 08481/493/506/76/651/83/756/70/86/92/98/801/19/22/8/30/54/900/32/41/53/55/57/93 and 09001/3/8/13/5/7/105/7/203 at the once great depot. Activity at Canton continued, but was dealt a fatal blow when the Royal Mail transferred its remaining postal services to road in 2004. EWS downsized and subsequently the bulk of Canton's staff were transferred to Margam where facilities were enhanced through a short extension to the shunter bay, along with the installation of a 2.5 ton pendant-controlled overhead crane. Other staff were moved to a newly opened fuelling facility at East Usk Yard in Newport, and the stabling point at Godfrey Road, Newport was closed. As EWS was still contracted to provide Class 37s to Arriva Trains Wales for the peak hour and Saturday Cardiff to Rhymney loco-hauled services, it continued to service them around Canton's 'ground lathe', and the locos would then stable, with the stock, in the carriage shed until required. When the Rhymney contract ceased, the remaining EWS part of the depot closed as a maintenance centre on December 10, 2005. The servicing shed and main shed were subsequently leased first to Pullman Rail and now Colas Railfreight, while the carriage shed and DMU are run by ATW.

The Pullman Rail engineering firm was founded by Mr Colin Robinson and it utilised the depot until the company was acquired by Colas, part of the French multinational Bouygues Group. Pullman Rail's work mainly involved rolling stock and component overhaul and the firm employed approximately 130 people and had a turnover of £10.6m in 2011/12. The deal saw enhancements and developments at Canton to allow it to become a strategic part of the Colas business in Wales and the UK.

Two Class 47s (47074 and 47107) flank a grubby Class 37 37180 by the old water tower in 1976. Cardiff Station is in the background.

Green liveried with full yellow end, Class 47/0 47094 stands in front of the servicing shed in 1975.

Depots Today

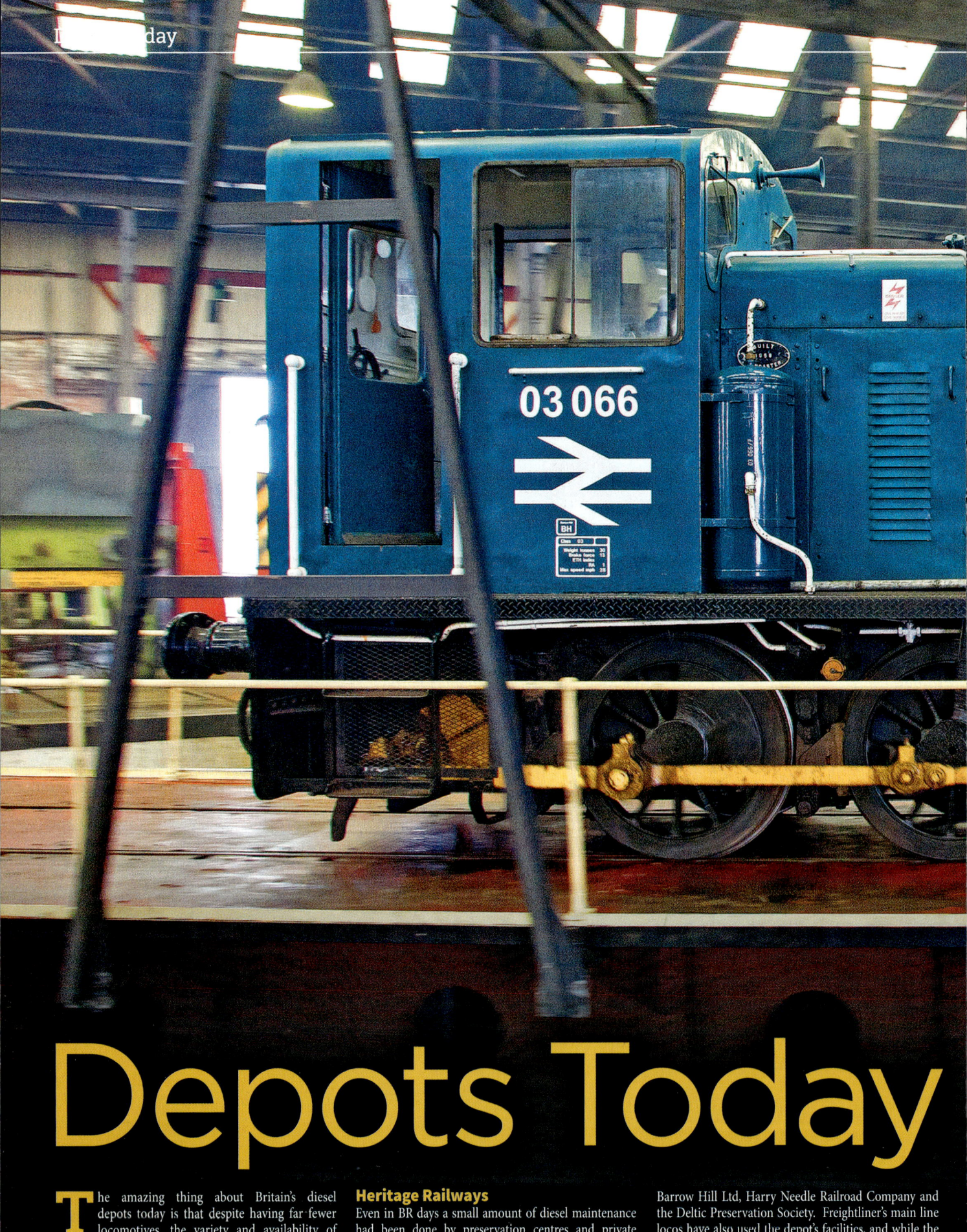

The amazing thing about Britain's diesel depots today is that despite having far fewer locomotives, the variety and availability of well-equipped facilities is as good, if not better, than it has ever been. While recent years have seen DB Cargo close many of its depots and maintenance facilities, several of them have gone on to find new leases of life. Freightliner, GB Railfreight, Colas Railfreight and Direct Rail Services have all grown and opened or re-activated old facilities to cater for their expanding businesses.

Heritage Railways

Even in BR days a small amount of diesel maintenance had been done by preservation centres and private concerns, but from privatisation and into the 2000s, independent providers flourished. Preservation centres such as the Midland Railway Centre repaired BR locos in the early 1990s and it's amazing to think that there were ever concerns when Barrow Hill Roundhouse was saved from demolition more than 20 years ago, over whether it could be filled with locos again. The site is now home to several loco owners, along with buildings used by Barrow Hill Ltd, Harry Needle Railroad Company and the Deltic Preservation Society. Freightliner's main line locos have also used the depot's facilities, and while the roundhouse is predominantly a preservation site it is also the embodiment of the modern multi-user diesel depot.

Thanks to the growing ranks of preserved diesels, many heritage lines have servicing and maintenance depots on a par with, if not better than, many of BR's early efforts. For example, at Kidderminster on the Severn Valley Railway, there is now a fully equipped three-road maintenance shed providing 1,000m2 of space for

Depots Today

ABOVE: Barrow Hill roundhouse near Chesterfield was once a sub-shed for Tinsley under BR, but today is thriving as both a preservation centre and also for private companies such as HNRC. Resident Class 03 03066 shunts a preserved brake van on to the turntable on December 10, 2016. (Robert Falconer)

up to four large locos. Contractor C21 Construction of Ludlow completed the building in November 2015. Having taken inspiration from Old Oak Common depot, it has lifting jacks, two inspection pits and a 10 tonne overhead travelling crane, making it the best-equipped diesel facility on any UK heritage railway. The total cost of the project is said to have been in the region of £800,000 and it was officially opened on May 20, 2016. Today there are a host of private well-equipped depots with a main line connection, or the ability to take a loco by low loader, that are able to offer services to main line operators.

Reactivated sites

In 2011, the former Burton Wagon Works became the home of Nemesis Rail. EWS closed the facility on December 28, 1996 and it then became a warehouse distribution depot devoid of a rail connection. Nemesis Rail runs the two road, 90m-long former wagon works as a diesel depot-come-carriage and wagon works repair centre. With a connection directly on to the Derby to Birmingham main line it has jacks capable of lifting vehicles up to 120 tons, a paint shop, fully compliant and auditable management systems, overhaul and return to service, routine maintenance, out of course emergency call out and repairs, fault finding and repair, major and minor component exchange, wheelset and motor changes, vehicle modification, specialist vehicle modification and build and, finally, power unit overhaul, from light repair to full strip down. All of these capabilities combine to make Burton a very comprehensive facility.

Leicester is another East Midlands depot to enjoy a revitalisation. It closed to steam on June 13, 1966, but beside its roundhouse was a newly built diesel depot. Initially a maintenance facility it was a mere fuelling point by 2008, and was subsequently closed by DBS. In 2013, Mark Winter and Edward Stevenson formed UK Rail Leasing and took out a three-year lease on the depot. It is now home to a growing fleet of Class 56s and other main line locos as the firm seeks to become an independent locomotive provider to third party operators. The facility has enabled companies such as Rail Operations Group to enter the stock transfer and spot-hire markets without any fixed depots of their own. ROG's fleet of two Class 37s, which are leased from Europhoenix, and five Class 47s, which they own, are maintained under contract with UK Rail Leasing, while fuelling and basic exams may be done wherever is convenient.

DB Schenker used its closed Crewe Diesel Depot as a secure storage site for many of its Class 56s, 58s and 60s. After a decade out of use the depot had badly deteriorated, but by early 2014 it was cleared and leased to Locomotive Storage Limited. A new roof was constructed, internal fittings and staff amenities renovated, and a 5 ton crane and heavy lifting jacks were re-installed along with partition screens in a similar manner to when the depot first opened, to prevent dust and dirt from infiltrating the maintenance area. LNWR Heritage came to the depot in

THE DIESEL DEPOT | 97

Depots Today

The Severn Valley Railway officially opened its newly built diesel depot on May 20, 2016. The following day D1062 Western Courier, *Hymek D7029, Network Rail's Class 73 73951* Malcolm Brinded *and Class 08 D3022 graced the impressive facility.* (David Bissett)

2015 to overhaul steam locos – a fulfilment of its original design purpose some 60 years after it was first conceived.

The freight companies
From humble beginnings at Sellafield with nuclear flask trains, DRS has expanded its original refurbished Class 20 fleet to include 33s, 37s, 47, 57s and new build 66s and 68s. Alongside its main facility at Carlisle it opened Crewe Gresty Road in 2007, utilising the former GWR two-track wagon works that opened around 1905. The building was totally refurbished with a new roof clad in corrugated sheeting and was re-opened on March 23, 2007.

Advenza Freight was purchased by Cotswold Rail in 2005, and with a valid safety case it was able to operate freight services. Cotswold Rail leased the closed Gloucester Horton Road Depot from 2006. Although it had last been used in 1992, it provided an ideal facility to house the company offices and stable its small fleet. Sadly, due to unpaid taxes, HM Revenue & Customs applied to the courts to have Advenza Freight wound up in October 2009, and after Cotswold Rail entered voluntary administration in January 2010 the company is now defunct. Other operators include British American Railway Services, which hires out its locos to other operators.

Colas has a fleet of classes 37, 47, 56, 60, 66 and 70, with maintenance facilities at Cardiff Canton and Washwood Heath. The Harry Needle Railroad Company owns a large number of locos that are hired to industrial users or main line operators. The company is able to undertake maintenance, repairs and heavy overhauls at its Barrow Hill facility. MiddlePeak Railways also offers locos, mainly specialising in Class 08s. West Coast Railways has its headquarters in Carnforth, but also operates out of the former Great Western Railway Depot at Southall Railway Centre in West London, while for half of the year it also uses part of Fort William Depot for the Jacobite service.

In 2013, GBRf opened its new Roberts Road Locomotive Maintenance Depot in Doncaster. It was built by Nobles Construction for Electro-Motive Diesel, which uses it to maintain GBRf's Class 66 fleet. Existing tracks and buildings were demolished to make way for the two buildings, with a Kingspan composite roof system and cladding throughout. The 75m by 32m shed holds four locos and has an integral overhead travelling crane capable of lifting out engine and transformer sets, along with two sets of 40 tonne jacks for lifting locos clear of their bogies. The second shed accommodates the washing apron and an under-floor wheel lathe with re-profiling mechanism.

The recent collapse of the coal market has hit Freightliner and DB Cargo incredibly hard. In response, the changing market DBC announced a re-organisation that could see up to 893 positions affected. Its depot requirement was also examined, and after previous closures and transfers of many of its sites to Arriva only Toton survived as a large depot, and even that is a shadow of its former self. Although DBC built a new facility at Bescot, virtually all of its heavy maintenance on its fleet of Class 60s, 66s and 67s is concentrated at Toton, and while its future seems secure 2016 marked another massive blow from which it may never recover.

Freightliner has maintenance facilities at Leeds Midland Road, Hope and York, along with train crew facilities at Taunton, Eastleigh, Bristol, Bristol North, Reading, West Thurrock, Hoo Junction, Bedford, Rugby, Peterborough, Sandiacre, Garston, Guide Bridge, Earles Sidings, Rother Valley, Doncaster, Midland Road (Leeds), Humber (Immingham), Teesside, Tyne Yard, Carlisle, Mossend and Dunbar. Interestingly, in between trips in order to cut down on light engine movements, the company also stables its engines at places such Coalville Mantle Lane, on the same roads as the old BR depot, and Tunstead Sidings, but neither of these could be considered to be a depot compared to the stabling points of old.

Conclusion
Ultimately the way in which depots are run has also fundamentally changed. In most cases, the maintenance and operation of locos are two totally separate concerns. Locos may be owned, part owned, leased or short-term hired and, equally, an operator no longer needs a collection of strategically placed depots, for the market of the privatised railway has matured and developed into one that offers an array of options to any existing or would-be operator. This means that while Britain's diesel depots are nothing like as large or as numerous as those of the heydays, as a collection of new, old and reinvigorated, they do at least offer a surprising variety for the modern enthusiast.

98 THE DIESEL DEPOT
www.railwaysillustrated.co.uk